Supervision in Action

Supervision in Context series

Coaching & Mentoring Supervision: Theory and Practice by Tatiana Bachkirova, Peter Jackson and David Clutterbuck

Skills of Clinical Supervision for Nurses: A Practical Guide for Supervisees, Clinical Supervisors and Managers (Second Edition) by Meg Bond and Stevie Holland

The Social Work Supervisor: Supervision in Community, Day Care and Residential Settings by Allan Brown and Iain Bourne

Supervision in Action: A Relational Approach to Coaching and Consulting Supervision by Erik de Haan

Psychotherapy Supervision: An Integrative Rational Approach to Psychotherapy Supervision by Maria C. Gilbert and Kenneth Evans

Forthcoming

Supervision in the Helping Professions (Fourth Edition) by Peter Hawkins and Robin Shohet

Clinical Supervision in the Medical Profession: Structured Reflective Practice by David Owen and Robin Shohet

Supervision in Action

A relational approach to coaching and consulting supervision

Erik de Haan

Mc Graw Hill

Open University Press

Open University Press
McGraw-Hill Education
McGraw-Hill House
Shoppenhangers Road
Maidenhead
Berkshire
England
SL6 2QL

email: enquiries@openup.co.uk
world wide web: www.openup.co.uk

and Two Penn Plaza, New York, NY 10121-2289, USA

First published 2012

A catalogue record of this book is available from the British Library

ISBN-13: 978-0-33-524577-2 (pb)
ISBN-10: 0-33-524577-3 (pb)
eISBN: 978-0-33-524578-9

Library of Congress Cataloging-in-Publication Data
CIP data applied for

Typesetting and e-book compilations by
RefineCatch Limited, Bungay, Suffolk
Printed by Bell and Bain Ltd, Glasgow

Fictitious names of companies, products, people, characters and/or data that may be used herein
(in case studies or in examples) are not intended to represent any real individual, company,
product or event.

The **McGraw·Hill** Companies

Contents

And if anyone makes fun of us for going to school at our age, I think we should appeal to Homer, who says that 'Shame does not befit a needy man'. Let us, then, regardless of what may be said of us, join together in taking care of our own and the youths' development.

Plato, *Laches*

Series editors' preface

We welcome this excellent new book by Erik de Haan to the Supervision in Context series. It is a very useful follow up to the recent edited book in this series, *Coaching & Mentoring Supervision: Theory and Practice* by Tatiana Bachkirova, Peter Jackson and David Clutterbuck, and to *Coaching, Mentoring and Organizational Consultancy* by Peter Hawkins and Nick Smith (2006), both published by the Open University Press. While supervision has been established in many of the other people-related professions such as psychotherapy, counselling, social work and psychology for several decades, the development of specific models for supervision in coaching and organisational consultancy has been much more recent. The first research and the first book specifically on supervision for coaches, mentors and consultants was *Coaching, Mentoring and Organizational Consultancy* and the first training course specifically for supervisors of coaches and mentors did not start until 2003. Yet in the last 10 years much has been done to develop this fast-growing field, of which this book is the latest, very welcome addition. Erik de Haan has been one of the people central to the development of the field, providing supervision and training in supervision to coaches and consultants, primarily at Ashridge Business School.

A particular contribution of this book is the extension of coaching supervision approaches into the field of organisational consultancy, where the complexities of supervision are increased. Indeed, the supervision may be of a team of consultants all working within the same organisational client system, at multiple levels in the organisation and with many different types of interventions. This requires the supervisor to be adept in a wide range of multidisciplinary skills, from understanding business, organisational dynamics, leadership, change and organisational development to team coaching, individual coaching and account management.

Erik brings together his training in person-centered, humanistic and psychoanalytic approaches with his own development of a relational approach to both coaching and supervision, where supervision focuses on the relationship(s) between the coach or consultant and their client(s), the relationship between the coach or consultant and the supervisor, as well as the dynamic relationship between these two distinct relationships. Erik shows how core psychodynamic approaches to understanding relational dynamics, such as valency, transference, counter-transference and parallel process, can be used in the supervision process. He also provides a great wealth of illustrative vignettes of supervision in practice, thus linking theory, methodology, practice and reflection – which is a key aspect of the supervisory process.

Another key contribution in this book is the work written jointly with Michael Carroll on how supervision can address ethical issues and develop the ethical maturity of coaches and consultants. This focus is timely, with growing ethical challenges for many of the leaders and organisations which are the clients of the coaches and consultants who come for supervision. These practitioners frequently need help in addressing not only the client's ethical issues, but their own. Central to this is how their work can serve multiple stakeholders – the individuals being coached or consulted to, the teams they belong to, the wider organisation and the systemic context in which the organisation exists.

This series focuses on how to create, develop and sustain helping relationships, through providing good quality supervision to those who work broadly in the people and helping professions. Good supervision is the key link in helping practitioners connect what they learn in theory with what they learn and do in practice, and is therefore the core of all continuous personal and professional development. At its best it serves and benefits the professional who is being supervised, their clients, the organisations in which they work (and work for) and the development of the profession. In today's world, no helping professional can afford to be without supervision. This book provides an excellent frame for coaches, mentors and consultants to help them understand what they should be demanding as part of sustaining the quality and development of their practice.

Peter Hawkins and Robin Shohet
August 2011

Acknowledgements

This book is dedicated to my supervisors over the last few years – Susanna Taffler, Gideon Hadary and Mary Bradbury – and to my teachers in the field of supervision: professors Charlotte Sills, Michael Carroll and Peter Hawkins.

I would also like to thank the two illustrators who have contributed to this book: Danee Miller and Michelle Moore, who produced diagrams in Chapters 1 and 4 and Appendix A, and Richard Bamsey, who drew the illustrations at the start of each chapter and the introduction. Special thanks go to colleagues Elaine Robinson, David Birch and Michael Carroll, for their vital contribution to Chapters 4, 5 and 7 respectively. Chapters 4 and 5 are based on articles that we wrote together and that have appeared previously elsewhere. David Birch has also helped with an earlier version of Chapter 1. Finally, my colleagues Liz Wiggins and Andrew Atter have contributed to the models and methods in Chapter 6.

Erik de Haan
www.ashridge.org.uk/erikdehaan
erik.dehaan@ashridge.org.uk

Introduction: metaphors for supervision

SUPERVISION AS...
The utility room

When we spend an afternoon working in the garden, weeding, digging, pruning, sowing, planting etc., and come indoors after the jobs are done, no doubt all sweaty and muddy, the first thing we have to do is take off our boots or shoes. Traditionally, our next port of call is the utility room or the bathroom, as a sort of intermediate space between the work in the garden and full participation in family life. Our hands are grimy, we need to wash them and possibly put on some cream. Our clothes are dirty or otherwise unsuitable for the activities we have planned for the evening, and we need to change out of them and back into our ordinary gear, our 'own' clothes.

Knowledge workers have another name for this intermediate space between work and home: *supervision*. Supervision is where we wipe the sweat from our brows and the dirt from our faces, wash our hands, look at ourselves in the mirror and get ready to become an 'ordinary' person again, without a 'role' or 'function'. To do so, we need to bring our newly acquired experiences, impressions and reflections up to the surface, review them and sometimes give them a clean, and then muster up the courage to process our emotions, undertake honest reflection and integrate our recent experience into our broader consulting practice.

For beginners, the utility room is a place to store their teaching books and the tools they are using less and less in their practice, and to grow seedlings and cuttings of their own ideas and opinions. Busy consultants use it as a place where they can leave behind all the paraphernalia of a hectic practice, to enable them come to themselves and finally 'examine things in depth'. Consultants with tough assignments and heavy responsibilities wash away spots and stains that belong not to themselves but to divided, despondent or angry organisations and clients. Consultants who have been put to the test and have had to take difficult decisions use the utility room to check if they still have dirt on their faces, and see if they can expunge their feelings of guilt and shame through the application of solvents.

Supervision can be defined as *disciplined reflection-in-relation wherein case history and principles are transformed into new potential for action and skills* (after Rapoport 1954). Supervision is therefore a process in which new practical knowledge is generated while taking account of (ethical) principles. Practical knowledge is nothing other than an 'irreversible change in potential actions' (De Haan 2004).

Underestimation is a major risk in organisation consulting and coaching practice. Unlike gardeners, deep-sea divers, police officers and many other caring or exploring professions, consultants and coaches don't need any special equipment to do their work – although it's not unusual for consultants to catch themselves unconsciously picking out clothes in an effort to fit in with the organisation they're going to visit. A uniform or protective clothing is a constant reminder of the role and the risks involved. Consultants usually lack such a reminder, so the risks of role uncertainty are much greater. As a result we forget far too easily the extent to which we expose and hurt ourselves, or invite hurt, in the consulting professions. We can then develop a 'thick skin' and disparage the constant stream of emotions that bombard us, such as enthusiastic promises, vain hope, defeated expectations, direct or indirect rejections, disguised criticism or jealousy, temptations to over-promise etc. – or act as though we don't need any help and can bear and process all of it by ourselves. However, that is certainly not always the case: to process it all, we need the involvement of outsiders who have gone through similar experiences and can help us put our own into new contexts.

I have been in this profession for a good number of years now, clocking up thousands of 'flying hours', and I notice that my own idea of what constitutes 'good coaching' and 'good supervision' is actually getting simpler. Good coaching is simply observing what the client brings to the session and what is going on in the client and ourselves, and expressing some of those observations from time to time. Good supervision goes a step further: besides expressing what we observe, we offer up more interpretations and sometimes even advice. Despite the fact that good consulting and coaching sessions are very simple and very easy to recognise, over the years I have seen the most experienced of consultants – myself included – struggle to achieve this standard. Looking back, my colleagues often tell me that what helped them most in the some ten years that it takes to acquire the right skills, was *supervision* with a trusted supervisor.

This book charts the entire discipline of supervision in seven compact chapters covering:

1   Overview of the field: quality assurance through supervision.
2   Techniques for supervisors, during supervision sessions.
3   Reflective techniques for supervisees.
4   Supervision for consultants and within more complex organisation-consultancy assignments.
5   Supervision as it actually happens, with a case from my own practice.
6   Supervision methods for individual and group supervision sessions.
7   Supervision contracts and testimonies.

In the process of mapping out the entire landscape of supervision, we consider a series of metaphors, one of which is depicted in each chapter by illustrator Richard Bamsey:

1   The tripartite role of the supervisor: gatekeeper, nurse, developer.
2   Supervision as parallel process handling, juggling echoes and parallels from other sessions.
3   Supervision as a beacon of reflection floating on a sea of complexity.
4   Supervision as shadow consulting, moving with, but shielded from, the scorching light of the assignments themselves.
5   Supervision as a torment of Tantalus, where each discovery comes too late to be used.
6   Supervision as two rather frightened people who have no idea about what's coming next.
7   Supervision as a recursive process, with reflection on reflection, a relationship that reflects other relationships, and a contract that refers to itself time after time.

In spite of the multiple layers of supervision and the abundance of meanings, a number of connecting threads keep recurring in this book. First, there is the importance of registering your own emotions or the 'affect' of the session, and of recognising parallel processes that carry new information under the surface of the relationship. Second, there is a 'growth spiral' which runs from doubt to tension, to the discovery that usually comes too late (see the concept of *l'esprit de l'escalier* in Chapter 5), to compassion and resignation, to new actions and interventions, to new doubts and tensions, and so on, all over again.

The seven chapters of the book are followed by two appendices as a deeper exploration for supervisors who want to go further. The first examines the roots of our modern thinking in terms of parallel processes – i.e. the discovery of the phenomenon of 'transference' and how this phenomenon has to be rediscovered over and over again in 'helping' relationships. The appendix describes a number of patterns that we can expect to see in such relationships. The second appendix focuses on the effectiveness of 'helping' conversations and what is known about that. It briefly outlines the results of quantitative research in supervision, coaching, counselling and psychotherapy, and summarises the importance of these results for supervisors: what freedom can we allow ourselves in our interventions, and what dimensions merit special attention in order to increase the likelihood of a better outcome? The link between these two appendices and with the rest of the book is the importance of the quality of the supervisory *relationship*, as a sanctuary for uncompromising reflection, as a platform for experimentation and as a source of insight into things going on in other relationships.

As organisation consulting and coaching have started to focus more on personal development and psychological aspects of leadership, authority and collaboration, supervision of consultants and coaches has expanded enormously. It is extremely important that the organisation consultant and coach are fit and able to handle the confidential and delicate issues arising from work organisations. Supervision is the most important tool of quality assurance for consultants and thus the best guarantee of quality and fitness we can give.

In the many examples of supervision featured in this book, I have carefully distinguished the three main parties of supervision with the words 'supervisor', 'supervisee' and 'client' – i.e., the word 'client' does not normally refer to the supervision client as that could be confusing. The word 'supervisee' is used throughout for this reason. As far as possible, I have resisted the temptation to serve up again various aspects from adjacent disciplines – such as counselling, consulting, mentoring and coaching – which are also relevant to supervision. I have confined myself as much as I can to phenomena and methods that are typical of and unique to supervision and supervisors. All of the examples come from my own supervision practice and that of a number of close colleagues, and not from border territory. I have done my very best to render case examples anonymous. I have asked permission for as many case examples as I could. Nevertheless, it is possible that the people in a case may recognise themselves, but I trust that they will also know that outsiders or colleagues will not be able to do so. After consultation with the consultants concerned, some cases were considered too sensitive but may be included in a subsequent edition. I am well aware of the ethical implications of publishing real-life case material, however, it is impossible for supervisors to continue learning if they can't do so on the basis of written case material. The longest case in the book, which takes up nearly all of Chapter 5, has been rendered completely anonymous and was worked out with the supervisee herself, Elaine Robinson.

Another important field that is not considered in this book – because it was explored previously in my 2004 book *Learning With Colleagues* – is that of peer consultation, co-coaching and action learning: the 'utility room' not hosted by an independent supervisor but designed by a number of colleagues working together. For me, supervision is quite different from peer consultation: a colleague is wholly on your side and has qualms about saying certain things; he[1] wants to spare you, and pulls punches. A colleague, however close, cannot really shake off all of their rivalling and competitive urges. Unlike a 'co-learning colleague', a supervisor *can* operate truly independently, and that's often just what you need as a consultant. In my experience, a combination of all three (individual and group supervision, and consultation with like-minded colleagues) is crucial during a consultant's career for real balance and effectiveness in that role.

---

[1] In the interests of legibility, almost all consultants, coaches and supervisors in this book are male. For 'he', 'him', etc., also read 'she', 'her' and so on.

1 Supervision as quality assurance: strengthening nested relationships

SUPERVISION AS...
Guardian – Nurse – Developer

Only a few years ago, it was common practice to set yourself up as an organisation consultant or executive coach based on the sole credentials of years of experience in business. Qualifications were unheard of and very few organisations thought to ask for them. All that is changing: most large corporations now make use of internal and external consultants and coaches, who are expected to have been trained in organisational development or organisational psychology, and accredited by a recognised institution. A parallel can be drawn with senior managers, who for decades have been under increasing pressure to continue their professional development with an MBA or a reputable leadership programme.

However, the achievement of a consulting or coaching qualification in itself cannot be taken as evidence of professionalism and competence. Organisation consultancy and coaching are extremely demanding activities which generally involve taking decisions in isolation while struggling with ethical dilemmas or invitations to collude with dysfunctional organisational behaviour. For this reason, it makes more sense to expect coaches and consultants to expose themselves to regular supervision – like social workers and therapists, for example. Together with continuing practical experience, supervision is a minimum requirement for maintaining professional accreditation. Supervision is no longer something that is 'nice to have'; it is becoming an essential prerequisite for maintaining quality, competence and profession-alism within organisation consultancy and coaching, as witnessed by a recent growth in books about supervision in the coaching and consulting professions (e.g. Bachkirova *et al.* 2011; Passmore 2011).

Supervision for consultants and coaches

Supervision for coaches and consultants is organised in small groups or on a one-to-one basis (see Chapter 6 for some state-of-the-art methods of supervision). Its purpose is to help coaches and consultants bring the very best of themselves to their work with clients. In practical terms this means ensuring that coaches or consultants are suffi-ciently well resourced to help their clients take responsibility for their behaviour and choices (or for what they don't do) at work. Viewed in that light, supervision is predom-inantly a developmental process. It can also be seen as a process for improving the quality of the work of the coach or consultant, including quality control and assurance. By attending to their own emotional and intellectual 'fitness', coaches and consultants will be in a stronger position to help their clients.

The first and most essential 'service' that supervision renders is the regular provi-sion of a safe and confidential space where the coach or consultant is helped to reflect on his professional practice. Coaches and consultants are often very busy, working to tight schedules, changing role frequently depending on the session or assignment, and do a lot of their work on their own and under considerable commercial pressure, in terms of both making and maintaining contacts. Taking time to reflect and to scrutinise one's own professional practice is often challenging, but it is well worth the effort, with potentially crucial benefits for clients.

CASE EXAMPLE

An experienced executive coach was working with a client who was about to become a father and who felt under intense pressure, both at home and in his leadership role. The coach had been working with the client for some time and they had built up a strong trust.

During the early sessions, the client hardly expressed any emotion but was now sharing immense anxiety, profound anger and a sense of helplessness. The coach felt overwhelmed by his client's strong feelings and was concerned that working with this level of emotion was beyond his competence. At the same time, he realised that the client was relying on their trusted relationship as one of very few places to bring his despair.

During supervision, the coach started processing his own emotional response to his client and discovered to his surprise that he was feeling protective towards him. With this insight and the encouragement of his supervisor, he felt strong enough to offer his client a clear boundary that would enable him to explore his emotions in a more detached way. The supervisor and coach agreed that if he felt he or his client was not coping, he would contact the supervisor directly in between sessions. That turned out not to be necessary.

I see supervision essentially as a quality assurance process for coaches and consultants, designed to give the outside world the confidence that the consultant or coach is 'fit for purpose', equipped with the insight, skills and personal resourcefulness to be able to help. The outside world includes close colleagues of the client or clients, but also future clients, fellow consultants and managers.

The frequency and duration of supervision varies according to the consultant's experience and workload but, as a rule of thumb, I assume that experienced coaches and consultants will need a minimum of five supervision sessions a year. My own organisation monitors this by updating our registration annually in terms of coaching, training and supervision hours. Less experienced consultants and coaches generally require more supervision, certainly once every four to six weeks in a busy practice. Supervision contracts can be of long duration and supervision can continue satisfactorily for many years, but it can also be very short, in the form of a one-off session organised as required.

A supervisory relationship generally develops over time, gradually including more of the supervisee's personal qualities and blind spots. Slowly but surely, the supervisee builds a capacity to observe himself in action and the discipline to reflect on his own work. The supervisee builds up what Casement (2002) calls an 'internal supervisor'. Over time the supervisee learns how to detach himself from the intensity of the moment in client relationships so that he can monitor what is happening between the client or clients and himself. As he does so, he increases his repertoire of responses to the moment itself, allowing himself a fraction more time to think before responding to a client's contribution. This in itself is very valuable because even a brief deferral of judgement can make a huge difference in a hectic day-to-day consultancy practice.

Consultants and coaches also learn gradually to trust their supervisor enough to share 'sensitive' issues from their own practice, including ethical dilemmas, strong feelings towards their clients and existential doubts about their own abilities. For example, they may be concerned that they have given a client overly harsh feedback. Perhaps they feel they have been too open or familiar with a client. Or they may be worried about a client's stress levels, alcohol consumption or mental health. Whatever the dilemma or issue, it takes courage to 'share' the material with a supervisor, but a confidential supervision session always provides an opportunity for fresh reflection. It also provides the independent perspective of an experienced colleague.

The supervisory relationship has traditionally been seen as a mixture of three essential relationships which I will associate here with developing, gatekeeping and nursing (see Kadushin 1976 and Proctor 1988 for earlier descriptions, and Hawkins and Smith 2006 for an earlier application in the field of coaching supervision).

The developer

Within a *developing* relationship (Kadushin's educational and Proctor's formative supervision), the supervisor focuses on giving a personal summary of the situation, including patterns and connections within the 'material' brought in. He bases this summary on careful observation of:

- the case material contributed;
- the person who is contributing: the supervisee;
- his own relationship with the supervisee;
- himself and his own emotions.

By sharing openly and frankly what seems to be going on, and 'on whose part' – i.e. who seems to have what involvement in the situation – the supervisor helps the supervisee in his self-development. The supervisee examines his own practice, recalls his own successes, doubts and failures, and identifies how he can tackle things differently and better. The supervisee also develops a fresh and more objective perspective on his own case material and practice, and a longer-term aspiration for his career.

The gatekeeper

Within a *gatekeeping* relationship (Kadushin's administrative and Proctor's normative supervision), supervisor and supervisee are 'gatekeepers' of the profession, often more so than the professional organisation of which the consultant or coach is a member. The supervisor fulfils this role more than the supervisee's line manager as well, because he is closer to this consultant's practice and the actual work done with and for the clients. The supervisor has to trust in what he hears in the supervision sessions. This means that the gatekeeper's role is limited to what the supervisee decides to share in supervision and what else the supervisor can find out during sessions. It is nevertheless an important function, which is often formalised in an annual 'testimonial' in the shape of a letter to the organisation employing the supervisee. Where necessary, in exceptional circumstances, this letter can be withheld and the supervisor can declare the consultant/coach unfit to practise. By communicating openly and clearly in the event of potential conflicts with major stakeholders or with the applicable professional codes, the supervisor helps the supervisee remain alert to his own contribution and responsibilities for clients and for the profession as a whole.

The nurse

Within a *nursing* relationship (Kadushin's supportive and Proctor's restorative supervision), supervisor and supervisee look after the supervisee in a more restorative sense: simply taking the time and space to think about current practice, which leads to greater serenity and reassurance. If a coach or consultant is truly exhausted or stressed by his work, the supervisor can bring attention to this and help to find a better balance. Through careful, supportive and encouraging interventions, the supervisor helps the supervisee to tackle his own practice in a more integrated way and with greater energy.

As a developer, the supervisor promotes learning within the organisation or coaching practice, by finding new angles and new solutions to tricky issues, and by broadening the supervisee's repertoire of possible interventions, while, as a gatekeeper and nurse, he is concerned with 'border disputes':

1   The supervisor-gatekeeper focuses on professional and ethical boundaries – i.e. on the instances where the relationship between supervisee and client(s) may go beyond the strict bounds of the consultancy relationship (and, similarly, the relationship between supervisee and sponsor(s) where it goes beyond the strict bounds of the contractual relationship).

2   The supervisor-nurse focuses on the boundaries that the supervisee imposes on himself, boundaries between the consultant or coach and the private person, the professional in the role and the professional outside the role. This therefore concerns those moments or times when the consultancy practice poses a risk to the practitioner's own balance or health.

The first role, that of developer, is always important and normally recedes into the background only temporarily when one of the other roles comes to the forefront. The three roles are normally in competition: they don't go together well at the same time, but they can build on one another. The supervisory process itself may bring about new tensions which may call for the 'nursing of wounds'. The gatekeeper's role also leads frequently to blocks and defensive reactions, which may be followed by more restorative and developing interventions.

A supervisor's field of work is broad, therefore, and has consulting and managerial elements. It also comprises elements of counselling. Experience and qualifications as a consultant or coach are therefore a prerequisite, and a background in counselling or psychotherapy is highly recommended. However, it is not necessary to have experience in the supervisee's field of expertise: supervisees can always explore more content-related issues further with a colleague in their own field.

Time after time, we are struck by the fact that the supervisor is in effect a living paradox because he combines so many opposing elements in his role (Kadushin 1976): he is both a guard and a developer, both a giver of feedback and a facilitator of self-evaluation, both wounding in his keen observations and a nurse of professional wounds, both an expert and a novice (because every case is a new one), both facilitative and authoritative, both a non-directive counsellor and a directive adviser.

My own approach to supervision is predominantly relational and client-focused (de Haan 2008a), meaning that I try constantly to devote attention to the supervision relationship as it develops. Patterns and phenomena in that relationship, which often have their origins in transference (see Appendix A), help to illustrate what may be going on in the case material – i.e. in the supervisee's consulting or coaching relationships. The relational supervisor is therefore ever-alert to possible 'parallel processes' between the supervision relationship and the supervisee's client relationships (see Chapter 2). A relational supervisor constantly asks himself if the way in which the supervisee achieves successes, finds himself at a loss for options or is plagued by doubts in his practice, bears similarities to this relationship, here and now, between supervisor and supervisee.

Being client-focused in supervision means that the supervisee's clients are constantly centre-stage and that the supervisor always reserves a central place in his thoughts for the needs of those 'end users' of supervision. And by being interested in the supervisee's physical and psychological condition, the supervisor ensures that the supervisee provides the best possible attention and service to clients.

CASE EXAMPLE: A PARALLEL PROCESS

The coach was a British management consultant who had been working in Italy, where he was coaching a local manager. In group supervision, he described how he struggled to relate to the exuberance of his client and he worked with another participant to explore how the Italian was challenging him.

At the end of their conversation, the supervisor drew attention to a 'parallel process': the fact that the coach's behaviour had changed to become animated and lively. After feeling almost intimidated by his client, this coach had proceeded to behave in the very same manner. This insight freed him sufficiently to genuinely enquire into what his client was communicating both verbally and non-verbally. It seemed surprising that he had first felt almost intimidated by his client and was now doing the very same thing to someone else.

I have seen the behaviour described in the above case example many times, both in supervision and in coaching. It seems to me to be an unconscious way of learning that helps us to handle strange behaviour by first adopting that same behaviour ourselves – a form of mimicry easily observable in primates and young children as well.

A relational model of supervision

The supervisor and supervisee work by means of conversations within an evolving supervision relationship that reflects on the supervisee's case material and working relationships. In the same way, the supervisee and his clients work by means of conversations within an evolving consulting or coaching relationship that reflects on the supervisee's clients' case material and working relationships. Much of the power and effectiveness of supervision lies in the fact that the latter relationships are reflected in the former,[1] with the possibility of making new discoveries in supervision relationships about your client relationships and even about relationships between your clients.

A relational perspective on supervision draws on everything that is known about the effectiveness of helping relationships, working alliances and parallel processes (see Appendix B and De Haan 2008a), and consequently focuses on the themes, issues and patterns of the interaction within the supervision relationship.[2] Relational supervision makes the following basic assumptions:

---

[1] And vice-versa. For example, I have often had the experience of (unconsciously) attempting a consulting intervention that is almost identical to an intervention carried out by my supervisor with me.

[2] For an overview of the patterns of interaction in the form of 'games' that supervisor and supervisee may play with each other – i.e. for an overview of the defensive patterns that may come to the fore when the supervision itself becomes too painful or complicated – see the articles 'Games people play in supervision' (Kadushin 1968) and 'Games supervisors play' (Hawthorne 1975).

- The supervisor assumes that people are fundamentally motivated to enter into relationships with others, so that much of what the two of them (as supervisor or supervisee) hope to achieve with this relationship is to repeat earlier relational patterns and, by reflecting on those patterns, to improve their relationships, both within and outside the confines of the meeting.
- The supervisor attempts to understand the material contributed by the supervisee from the angle of the relationships within and surrounding the case material. All content of supervision can therefore be regarded as relational.
- The supervisor endeavours to build a relationship that is as strong and productive as possible.
- The supervisor devotes explicit attention to the evolving relationship as a 'mirror' of, or 'laboratory' for, other relationships of the supervisee.
- The supervisor doesn't deny himself any specific interventions, regarding either the nature or the sequence of his own contributions. If the supervisor believes that a particular intervention suits his own personality, and can fully support it, then that choice is justified.

My supervision model builds on this relational perspective by mapping out the matrix of relationships around and within supervision, and the links between those relationships, including the parallels that can occur between pairs of relationships involving the same person.

In this model the emphasis is on the various relationships around and within supervision, relationships that may be separate in time or space but are closely interconnected in terms of emotions, thoughts and ideas. To model relationships between relationships, I have opted, since de Haan (2008a), for a 'ring model' of supervision. From time immemorial, rings have been a symbol of relationships – as in a wedding ring. Each ring in the model stands for a working alliance or work relationship, or even a personal relationship, and each ring can be seen from three perspectives:

1   What the 'client' may bring to the relationship (including transference – see Appendix A).
2   What the other party, i.e. the coach/consultant/supervisee, supervisor, colleague, facilitator, manager etc., may bring to the relationship (including counter-transference – see Appendix A).
3   What is going on at any time between the two (in other words, the process, the 'in-between' or the product of what both parties bring).

The supervision session is of course centred around the supervisee's agenda. The supervisee exposes his own practice, and hence himself, to supervision in order to shine a new light on it, and to equip himself to tackle it as effectively as possible. This is why we can put the relationships of the supervisee's *clients* at the centre, and regard all other relationships – such as the supervisee's consulting relationships, or the supervision relationship here and now – as sources of reflections and perspectives on those central relationships.

How can the supervisor help client relationships with which he has no direct contact? First, the supervisor listens to an account of the supervisee's reflections on those relationships, as they appear to him here and now. He can then put forward his own observations and introduce a new perspective, or confirm, reassure, challenge, confront, etc. A survey of the main benefits that experienced coaches hoped to gain from supervision found that a new perspective, reassurance and suggestions were the 'top three' on their list (Day *et al.* 2008).

The supervisor uses his unique position as a participant-observer of a network of relationships to pick up new information, simply by being open to the way in which the story is told, what is going on between the participants in the session, and the way he feels. Often, the way in which things are contributed, and the gestures, expression, tone and feeling used by the speaker are just as informative as the actual words. By resonating with the tone and the music, the supervisor combines observations from both worlds, the relationship networks and the current session, thus arriving at new and incisive patterns (see also Chapter 2).

Figure 1.1 gives a concise summary of the ring model and shows how supervision interlinks many relevant relationships. This shows how the supervision session reflects

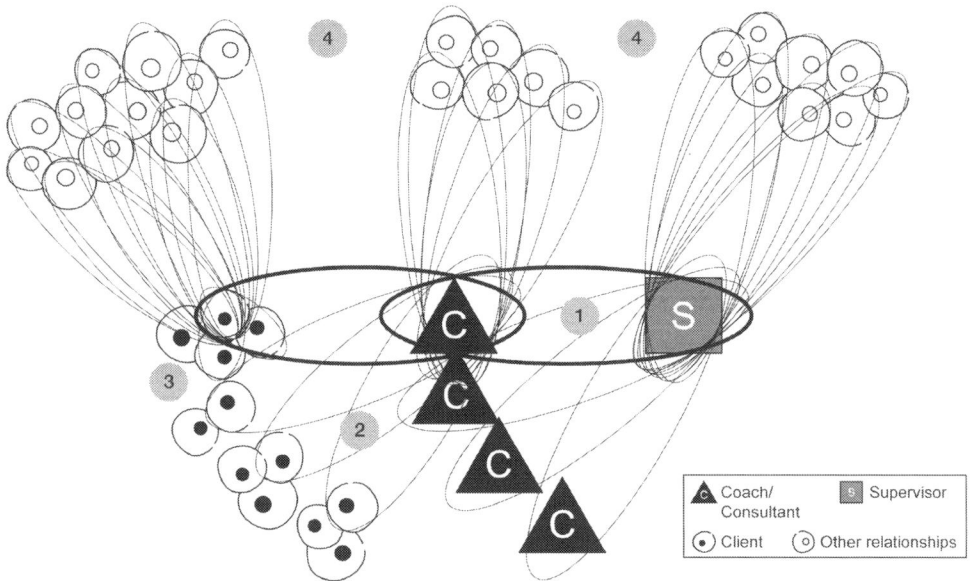

Figure 1.1 A relational summary of supervision.

Key
1   Stands for the supervisor's supervision relationship(s) which are present in the room in group supervision or not in individual supervision.
2   Stands for the client relationships of the consultant or coach receiving supervision. In general, one of these relationships, or a coherent group of relationships, takes centre-stage during supervision.
3   Stands for the organisational relationships of the client(s) of the consultant or coach which play a role in the case material under discussion.
4   Stands for other and earlier relationships of the supervisee's client(s), the supervisee himself and the supervisor. All of these relationships in the lives of clients, supervisees and supervisors may be relevant to the supervision session and the outcome of supervision.

the consultancy relationship being discussed at a given moment, and how reflections and resonances of other client relationships of the supervisee can also play a role. At least five relevant perspectives can be identified for each supervision issue:

a   Relevant relationships of the supervisee's client.
b   Other relationships of the supervisee with which he can develop similar relationship patterns: current clients, in particular those in the organisation under discussion, previous clients, and other working or personal relationships. The main formative relationships are of course those with the supervisee's own caregivers, brothers and sisters.
c   The consultancy or coaching relationship introduced here and now by the supervisee.
d   The supervision relationship as it is developing here and now.
e   Other client and personal relationships of the supervisor.

Supervision links all of these relationships, like links in a chain, enabling supervisor and supervisee to observe them all and thus find new answers to questions within old patterns; new insights which may apply across all of these relationships or relationship networks.

CASE EXAMPLE

The relational nature of supervision is particularly apparent when you work with more than one supervisee on the same day. For example, if I look back on today, a busy day full of supervision sessions, I realise how different I was with the fairly serious, highly experienced, slightly older and more guarded Simone; with the bubbly, ever-optimistic and appreciative Sarah, who is around my own age and is completely present during our sessions but seems to make no headway at all in between times, so that the start of each session mirrors the one before; with the extremely successful but relatively insecure Leonard, who always makes me feel insecure and reflective in turn; with the slightly washed out but very sensitive John who, if I'm honest, always depresses me to an extent; or with the businesslike, stern and, in my eyes, critical and demanding Alexandra. All of these people encounter a different Erik. In conjunction with me, they co-create a relationship with an Erik who is unique – to both of us! This unique relationship goes to ground between meetings, only to resurface in its full intensity each time I see them again, or perhaps even sooner, when I start to anticipate their arrival in my office.

Figure 1.1 illustrates the complexity of the web of relationships that a supervision session explores. It is a rich spectrum of relational patterns that can be observed, interpreted and transformed into other patterns during supervision. We owe the ability to do this to the phenomenon of transference, which was first described by Freud in 1905 (see Appendix A). Without transference, the perspectives on a case contributed to a session are endless and therefore meaningless, because they are not bound together in coherent patterns. Without transference, moreover, relationships that are more distant from the case would have less of a bearing. Nothing could be more at odds with the experience during supervision. It is precisely the phenomenon of transference that makes us take account of the fact that coherent patterns recur and become reinforced between relationships, and that very 'distant' relationships, such as those with one's own brothers, sisters, ex-bosses and ex-partners, actually have a strong bearing. Relationships that were formed in a distant past and that now appear to have a minimal visible effect on the supervisee or the supervisee's clients can actually be vital to a sound understanding of the case material. Freud suggested in 1912 why transference phenomena are so important in 'helping' conversations. He defined transference as that part of a person's highly individual, personal and largely unconscious emotional wishes or impulses that is not satisfied in their current relationships. According to Freud, there are a few 'clichés' (or deep-rooted ways of approaching relationships) that we carry with us, that we continue to repeat throughout our lives precisely because they are never truly satisfied (Freud 1912). These frustrated impulses continue to express themselves in relationships, rather than in words or conscious thought, precisely because they remain unfulfilled and unconscious. It goes without saying that it can benefit supervisees – and their clients – enormously if these patterns are nevertheless picked up and put into words for them, provided this is done in a supportive and respectful way.

Parallel processes are the result of transference. The relational impulses that the supervisee brings to the supervision session are an invitation to a complementary relational response. With transference occurring in this supervision relationship, the relationship starts to mirror, or develop in parallel with, important earlier relationships, such as the relationship between supervisee and client(s) which is under discussion here and now, or with earlier helpers in the supervisee's life, or with significant figures who helped to make the supervisee the person he is. Within all possible parallel processes, the processes that are parallel to the case material being discussed during the supervision have a lead over the others, because the supervisee's thoughts are occupied with that particular consultancy or coaching relationship. This is why we often see that processes develop during supervision in a way that mirrors their development during the consultancy or coaching focused on in supervision, but now with the supervisee in the role of protagonist, while the supervisor attempts to maintain a listening and reflective presence. The most obvious parallel processes in supervision are those between the supervision session and the particular encounter spoken about by the supervisee, and those between that supervisee/client encounter and encounters between the client and others in the workplace. Digging slightly deeper, we often come across parallels between the supervisee or the supervisee's client in their recent sessions and their own formative relationships, such as those with caregivers, brothers and sisters. It is often safer and easier in supervision to highlight parallels between the client session conducted by the supervisee and other sessions or relationships of the client. It can take courage to reflect on possible parallels between the present, ongoing supervision session and other sessions of the supervisee, but those reflections are certainly worth the effort.

Parallel processes and transference are constant and ubiquitous. The supervisor is in a privileged position in terms of observing these processes, because he is at one remove from a wealth of parallels and can therefore comment on them more easily and more objectively. It is often the supervisor who notices parallel processes first, not because he has a special talent but mainly because he occupies a special position that allows him to view consulting and coaching relationships from a distance. The supervisee's position is that of a hinge or bridge, a linking pin or 'translator' between phenomena that are discovered during supervision and the context in which those phenomena tend to occur.

Despite the ubiquitous nature of transference phenomena, supervision remains a unique place for discovering them and holding them up to the light of enquiry. This is partly because the supervisor views the client situation from a distance, mediated by a supervisee with a presence in both the client situation and the supervision situation, and also because these parallel processes, in passing through the rings as depicted in Figure 1.1, are amplified and attenuated in a manner that is comparable to the transmission of music through different media such as water, wood or air: certain wavelengths are amplified and others attenuated, with the stronger tones becoming audible thanks to resonance, and the weaker ones being lost. In supervision, the participants themselves are the media that amplify or attenuate the parallel processes, or 'relationship waves'. The emergence and spread of parallel processes is therefore a highly personal and subjective process which depends hugely on who is present, which earlier relationship patterns these partners have experienced, which processes they pick up on easily and which fail to resonate with them, which of their own relationship patterns they can 'admit' to their conscious thoughts, etc. A different supervisor arrives at different parallel processes, precisely because he vibrates in response to different frequencies. These highly relational propensities for responding to, and connecting with, different group emotional patterns were described by Bion (1961) who called them 'valencies' (more about the phenomenon of valency in Chapter 4).

Supervision in work organisations

Increasingly, internal consultants within large organisations are interested in supervision, given the sensitive nature of relationships in their practice. For external consultants and coaches, it is often more natural to go in for quality assurance. Many a client organisation requires its external consultants and coaches to be in supervision, and some ask for a reference about supervision that includes, for example, the frequency of supervision sessions and the type of issues their consultant would bring to supervision. The client organisation can also request examples of the way in which the consultant or coach learns during supervision. Some client organisations take things a step further and interview the supervisor of their coaches and consultants[3] or require a 'certificate of competence' for each of their external coaches, written by their supervisor (for an example of a testimonial of this kind, see Chapter 7). Some organisations go even further and organise their own assessment centres for all coaches wishing to be on a shortlist for the organisation in question.

---

[3] Something that is often difficult for the supervisor, because how do you say something friendly and positive without letting anything slip about your supervisee? Confidentiality prohibits supervisors from talking about their supervisees. Often, the best option is not even to confirm that someone is your supervisee and wait for your supervisee to request the recommendation.

Other organisations prefer to provide supervision in-house, for both internal and external consultants. Group supervision can be an attractive option in this situation. Bringing coaches and consultants together in small groups (in a live session, or virtually) fosters a feeling of camaraderie and mutual support. In addition, learning within a community of organisation coaches or consultants is a good counterbalance to a professional's sometimes lonely and isolated practice.

There is also a potential organisational benefit from such group supervision, as the supervisor(s) will inevitably discover patterns that are common to many consultancy assignments within the organisation (as illustrated in Figure 1.1). Supervisors can help to feed back those patterns to the organisation, provided this is done on a non-attributable, anonymous basis (see also Chapter 4 and the example in Chapter 7).

But there are also risks associated with internal group supervision. These have to do with potential breaches of confidentiality, especially in situations where the consultants may know who is working with whom, as is often the case. These risks can be reduced by concluding a clear contract, but they are not always avoidable. If these risks cannot be avoided, it is better to opt for individual supervision. The bigger the organisation, the smaller these risks. I agree with Proctor (2008) that, provided the setting allows it, the advantages of group supervision generally outweigh the drawbacks. Other advantages of group supervision are the sharing of best practices by the different consultants, the possibility of simulating consulting or coaching sessions within the group to give participants live feedback on their way of working, and the increasing responsibility within a group context for the supervision itself and sometimes for the consultancy work within the organisation (if the group consists of consultants working on the same project).

If one consultant or coach is brave enough to expose a sensitive issue to the piercing gaze of his colleagues, or if one participant has mustered enough courage to express what everyone is thinking but no one has the nerve to say, others will normally be quick to follow suit. Group supervision within work organisations also has the advantage of being quite a bit more affordable for each participating consultant or coach.

For more on organisational supervision, supervision of complex consulting assignments and shadow consulting, see Chapter 4.

CASE EXAMPLE

A team of coaches working with 'high potential' leaders at a government department had been meeting virtually for group supervision. Over time it became apparent that the content of many of the coaching sessions was about the coachees' poor relationships with the executive team, with many of the coachees blaming senior management for being remote and uninterested. Some of the coaches themselves felt similarly about senior management and wanted the supervisor to feed the concerns back to the executive via the learning and development manager. The supervisor helped the coaches recognise that they were colluding with their clients and that they were perhaps part of a 'parallel process'. He then helped the coaches reappraise their role and the coachees' personal responsibility for their interaction with senior management.

What makes a good supervisor?

Hawkins and Shohet (2006) point out that one of the biggest obstacles to effective supervision is the supervisee's fear that he will be judged or criticised by the supervisor. Many empirical studies support this finding – i.e. that coaches do not bring all of their most pertinent issues to supervision, sometimes for fear that the process will be too painful or shaming for themselves, sometimes due to awe or a need to shield their supervisor from sensitive issues (see e.g. Lawton 2000; Gray *et al.* 2001; Day *et al.* 2008). Good supervisors are able to keep this problem constantly in mind. To this end, they focus on:

- putting supervisees at their ease;
- being open and clear about the importance of sharing information;
- showing appreciation of the fact that this 'plunge into the unknown' requires courage;
- familiarising supervisees with the supervision process;
- creating an environment that is as safe and confidential as possible and in which the supervisee feels understood.

Without this environment, it is unlikely that the supervisee is going to benefit from critical feedback or challenge.

Other qualities and attributes that we might hope to find in an 'ideal supervisor' are a passion for learning, flexibility, humour and an ability to see situations from multiple perspectives combined with a sensitivity to the wider organisational issues. For a group supervisor, we should add group process awareness and facilitation skills to our list.

CASE EXAMPLE

A coach and supervisor have worked together for four years, mainly over the phone, during which period the coach has changed her emphasis from outplacement to executive coaching. She speaks about her 'favourite' client and relates how he is very quick-witted and almost falls over his own words and ideas, which occasionally break into a stammer.

'It is as if he brings out the best in me. I feel I am more forthright and open. He listens attentively and builds on my words, and he changes his actions as a result. Do you have that sometimes, a client that reinvigorates you to such a degree?'

The supervisor answers affirmatively and they explore what makes working with this client feel so successful. The supervisor also suggests that, occasionally, when people talk that quickly and intensely, there may be a second purpose, quite contrary to bringing forth a multitude of ideas. That purpose may be to actively not think about certain other things and keep them out of awareness. A stammer may point to other, less welcome feelings and, as the supervisee is trained in psychodynamic counselling, he reminds her of the idea of 'conversion hysteria'. The coach becomes thoughtful and suggests she will offer still more space to the client to see if more can be expressed next time.

Summary

Accreditations, qualifications and other certificates of competence are only valid on the day they are issued. Successful accreditation, a sound educational background and ample practical experience are not the only factors that make up the quality of the consultant. The latter's quality is determined predominantly by the **quality of reflection** on his own work.

Supervision gives the consultant or coach a regular time and space for reflection, and a partner to mirror, broaden and deepen those reflections. This makes regular supervision the best form of **quality assurance** that we have for consultants, facilitators and coaches – and for supervisors themselves.

Supervision has three main functions:

1   **Developer** (formative): through careful observation, supervision helps to maintain a fresh, objective perspective on the supervisee's case material and practice.
2   **Gatekeeper** (normative): by communicating openly and clearly in the event of potential conflicts with other parties or with professional ethics, supervision helps the supervisee remain alert to his own responsibility for clients and the profession as a whole.
3   **Nurse** (restorative): through careful, supportive and encouraging interventions, supervision helps the supervisee to tackle his own practice in a more uniform way and with greater energy.

A **relational approach** to supervision optimises the use of the supervisory relationship itself, holding that:

- People are deeply motivated to enter into relationships and to repeat relationship patterns.
- Supervisory material benefits from exploration in terms of relationships around and within the case material.
- It is worthwhile to build a supervisory relationship that is as strong and productive as possible. The supervisor devotes attention to the evolving relationship as a 'mirror' and a 'laboratory' for other relationships of the supervisee, allowing both reflection and experimentation. The supervisor does not deny himself any specific interventions and associations, regarding either the tone or the structure of the session.

The relational approach leads to the **ring model of supervision**, in which different relationships are reflected in a supervision session:

- the supervisee's client relationships which are the focus of the case material;
- the supervision relationship as it is developing here and now;
- the relationships of the supervisee's client(s) which are centre-stage at this moment;
- other and previous relationships of the clients, the supervisee and the supervisor.

Advantages of group supervision within consulting projects and organisations:

- It explores relationship patterns that are common to the group of internal and external consultants of the organisation.
- Supervisees have an opportunity to share and learn from their best practices.
- Supervisees practise their own coaching and consulting skills during supervision.
- Supervisees in a group muster more courage and responsibility: where one takes the lead, others will follow.
- Group supervision tends to be less expensive than individual supervision.

2   Techniques of the supervisor: echoes of other relationships

SUPERVISION AS...
Echos and parallels

The case material discussed in supervision is an echo of a consulting or coaching assignment, mostly an echo from the past and sometimes a foreshadowing of the future. The case material therefore resonates by definition in this conversation with an event that has already taken place or is still to take place. This resonance or echo is distorted by the passing of time and by the specific emotional responses of the person giving the account, also described as 'valencies' (Bion 1961). Valencies are relational propensities for responding to, and connecting with, different group emotional patterns. Bion adopted this term from chemistry, where different chemicals have a different valency for interacting with other chemicals in certain ways.

The source of the echo is itself an echo of earlier echoes in other places, relationships and relationship patterns that have led to the specific situation. In supervision, the echo is captured, enhanced and listened to. The conversation offers a unique opportunity to allow the echo to continue to reverberate and to observe it in all its base notes and harmonics; a unique opportunity which itself in turn introduces new distortions and resonances arising from the specific relationship built up between supervisee and supervisor and from the highly personal resonances of both ('valencies'). Supervision provides an impartial, safe space where all of these echoes can be observed and explored. This is done in the first instance by listening closely.

Listening under the surface

What we can notice within the case material

Being able to listen closely and attentively is essential in all consulting professions, from expert advice to policy development, from coaching to facilitation. The role of the supervisor places special demands on the quality of listening in the sense that both 'content' and 'interaction' are vital. And to make it even more complicated, content and interaction are usually strongly intertwined in supervision sessions, so that the supervisor is constantly honing his skill in intuiting links between content and interaction.

For a supervisor, the whole complex of communications at content and interaction level is of eminent importance. On the one hand, he has to reflect on the case material together with the supervisee and, based on his own professional knowledge and experience, develop a well-founded opinion on the case and what his client, the supervisee, is doing in the case. On the other hand, it is at least as important that he is sensitive to the way in which the supervisee gives his account and the way in which the supervisee relates to him. To put it briefly, the supervisor must be sensitive to the way in which the relationship between himself and the supervisee develops while discussing the case material. The supervisor knows that what happens at this level of interaction can say just as much about the case as the information conveyed by the facts and content-related aspects. Later in this chapter we will examine a number of regularly recurring forms of interaction, of relationships between supervisor and supervisee.

How does this simultaneous listening to content and interaction work in the supervisor's practice? In my experience, listening to more than one aspect at the same time is impossible.[1] It is more a question of alternating our focus of listening, registering the following aspects from moment to moment:

1   Content of the case material (there and then).
2   Interaction level (here and now).

---

[1] Since von Helmholtz (1867) we have known that our conscious attention, be it spatial, visual or motor attention, is largely linear and exclusive. This means that our attention jumps from field to field, and so forms an immense bottleneck of around five 'things' that someone can focus on second by second – not at the same time, but sequentially.

3   Our own discoveries and emotions – in other words, our own surfacing insights at content and interaction level.
4   Our own other interests when we are distracted from the supervisee. If we are honest, we have to admit that however well a supervision session is going there are still moments, often mere fractions of a moment, when our attention is not focused on the conversation. It has strayed, for example, to the room we are sitting in, clothing, emails, things going on in our own lives, and so on.

It is important in supervision not to impose immediate self-censorship on these natural shifts in our attention. Imposing demands on our attention means that we narrow our focus and allow ourselves less scope for listening freely. As a consequence, it is not a good idea to impose rules on our listening, for example by asserting that content (layer 1) is most important during the introduction of a new case, or that being distracted from the case (layer 4) should be avoided at all times. All four alternating fields of attention may be relevant to the supervisee, and thus ultimately to the supervisee's client. It is usually the case that, even when you are distracted, there is something going on in you that is connected with what the supervisee is saying, or the way in which he is saying it. A feeling of hunger is different from a feeling of boredom, thinking about the next email is different from thinking about the previous supervisee, and each of these may be relevant to the case material in this room at this moment. To put it briefly, being distracted is not a bad thing: what matters is what you do about it. Often, when we are distracted for a moment, our thoughts return to the session in the form of a tendency to change the topic or structure of the conversation. Instead of giving in to that tendency, it can be useful to look at the roots of the distraction itself first: why now, at this moment? Was this due to boredom, irritation or a literal 'turning away from' my supervisee? The answers to such questions are often relevant to the case. Just as an idea about the case itself can be both relevant and irrelevant, being distracted from the case – or from the other person in the room – can be both relevant and irrelevant to the case material.

CASE EXAMPLE: BEING DISTRACTED

It's the first individual supervision session after coming back from holiday. The supervisor is feeling in good form but has to get back into the rhythm of work and the handling of this type of intensive session. It strikes him that he suppressed a yawn a couple of times during these first two hours of supervision and he wonders if his supervisee noticed that. The yawns always come when he himself believes a certain client assignment has been discussed enough and it is time to move on to the next one.

Right at the end of the session, the supervisee thanks him enthusiastically but then asks if he never gets tired of this work. The supervisor immediately makes the association with the two suppressed yawns and concludes that the supervisee must have picked up something from them. Instead of giving an honest answer, he hears himself say that, on the contrary, 'it is always fascinating to explore this sort of client material.' Right at the end of the session, when they are saying their goodbyes, he evidently can't find it in his heart to say something controversial such as, 'Yes, there are of course times when I wander off or feel my own tiredness coming over me.'

The four fields of attention are distinguishable but closely connected at the same time. Interaction (layer 2) often shines a new light on case material (layer 1), while one's own emotions (layer 3) can say something about interaction (layer 2). Being distracted (layer 4) often points to a suppressed emotion in ourselves (layer 3), such as boredom, irritation or a desire to be somewhere else, thus also providing information about the evolving relationship and the content of the case (layers 1 and 2). On the one hand, our attention is truly focused differently when it is concentrated on our own ideas or on the other person, on the case or on something outside supervision. On the other hand, the way in which our attention jumps from one level to another ties all of the threads together. When our attention jumps back to the case, it can often bring with it an inspiration drawn from another layer which effectively yields a new understanding of or perspective on the same case, an understanding that may be of vital importance for the supervisee himself, for his client or for the client's organisation, which is only indirectly a client of the supervision.

Another way to look at the various aspects of supervision and the shifts in our attention is to consider the multiple layers of communication in the account of content given by the supervisee. The following is a simple breakdown of layer 1 (the content of the case) that I find useful in supervision:

1a Content of the case material itself, such as background, issue, progress and salient events.
1b Emotions of the supervisee while giving his account, such as eagerness and enthusiasm or conversely tension, wariness and distraction.
1c Intentions of the supervisee while giving his account, such as the presence or absence of motivation for supervision, or apparent objectives of the supervisee here and now in presenting his material.
1d Metaphors, stammering, slips of the tongue, choice of words and other use of language.
1e Gestures and other non-verbal signals during the account.

Each of these five communication aspects can put us on the scent of what is going on in the case material. In addition, they can form bridges to the next layer, the level of interaction or relationship between supervisee and supervisor. For example, the supervisee's emotions and gestures at this moment often say something about how it feels for the consultant to work with this client or organisation and have a directly perceptible effect on the supervision relationship here and now, and hence on the nature of the interaction developing during supervision.

In a similar way, we can also make further distinctions within the other layers – for example, within the level of interaction we can distinguish between working alliance and transference phenomena. Bordin (1979) and others subdivided the working alliance further into agreement on the aims of the conversation, agreement on the interpretation of the task and strength of the rapport or connection between the participants.

It is worthwhile letting our attention jump not only between layers 1, 2, 3 and 4, but also within the levels of the account itself, which again often appear to be largely connected. Sometimes the emotions here and now reinforce the emotional side of the content of the case; sometimes emotions now appear to be in flat contradiction to what is going on in the case; and sometimes emotions are a form of commentary on the case, via concern, sympathy, empathy, irritation, frustration, etc. All of these possibilities may be important in gaining a better understanding of the case. The same is true for the supervisee's intentions in giving his account, and for the use of metaphors and gestures. As explained by Freud ([1904] 1924), slips of the tongue and awkwardness in speaking sometimes give an insight into a hidden, unconscious response, into what the supervisee is suppressing at this moment and leaving out of his account. The same is true for layers 3 and 4: if we as supervisors stammer or trip over our words, or haven't quite gathered our thoughts, it opens up new insights into what we are trying to suppress at that moment in time. The same is true to a lesser extent for metaphors and gestures: these aspects are also less consciously controlled than the clear, rational description of the case, or, on the part of the supervisor, his own astute, rational ideas about the case.

CASE EXAMPLE

An executive coach talks about an assignment in a large multinational organisation, an organisation where he is on the English 'coach short list' and receives a regular flow of clients as a result. This assignment concerns a young, bright manager from Hungary, whose initial request was for guidance in working within a different culture (that of the Netherlands). The coach has now had around five sessions with the manager, the contract has broadened somewhat and the results are positive.

During supervision, he says that his client has recently had a new boss, who early on asked for information about the coaching sessions, and ideally for reports from the coach after each session. The client made it clear to his new boss that a coach is not able to do that. The coach proposed a three-way meeting and has spoken recently with the boss. The manager refrained during this conversation from making the same requests he had made earlier with the client.

The coach clearly feels indignant about the new manager, about the demands he is placing on the coaching, about the pressure he is exerting on his client and about his perceived insincerity in not wanting to make the same demands to the coach directly. The supervisor plays certain significant uses of words back to the supervisee: 'lack of trust' and 'client feels bullied'. But as soon as he hears those words played back, the supervisee qualifies them ('It's not as bad as that'; 'That's not how I meant it'), causing the supervisor to say, not once but twice: 'I don't understand. What is this about?'

The supervision session takes on a difficult edge. The supervisee feels he isn't being helped or understood and the supervisor feels incompetent and inadequate. The session begins to resemble more of a discussion, the summaries are more like counter-arguments, and the supervisee seems to be making dismissive gestures.

It is only when the supervisor says that he feels 'pulled in' to the session, that he feels pressure to share a particular concept or opinion, and that there may be similarities with the pressure the supervisee feels in the organisation to adopt a particular position (protective with regard to his own coachee, defensive with regard to the coaching contract), that a reversal occurs in the relationship. It is only when the supervisor is able to identify the (possible) parallels in awkwardness and negative assessments – instead of becoming more and more distracted by his own irritation – that recognition dawns in the supervisee, together with a deep feeling of being understood and helped. The atmosphere in the session is now completely different and the coach realises that he has allowed himself to be tempted to start working outside the boundaries of his coaching contract and to start seeing his coachee's boss as a new client, or as a rival, who threatens to take the successful relationship with 'his' coachee away from him.

Despite the sublime richness of a supervision session,[2] which is reflected in case description and interaction, it remains crucial that we should continue to listen closely to ourselves as supervisors. Our own semi-conscious or bodily reactions to the 'material' in supervision often contain the key to a real understanding of what is going on at this moment within the supervisee, or in the organisation under discussion. Listening to ourselves also means listening to our own 'distraction' and to moments when we step outside, or are at risk of stepping outside, the role of supervisor.

What we can notice within the supervision relationship

Focusing on the level of interaction is probably the most important thing in supervision: supervisees are keen to learn about their client relationships and do that in a 'helping' relationship with a supervisor. The interaction level reflects the client relationships and other relationships of the supervisee, as we will see in the next section. Moreover, the interaction level is also the basis of the 'helping' relationship during supervision.

It is essential as a supervisor to be constantly aware that the ostensibly pleasant, polite, friendly and amicable supervisee–supervisor relationship conceals another relationship of a more hidden and distorted nature. That relationship is dominated by the satisfaction of needs and the avoidance of vulnerabilities by both professionals in the room. With experienced professionals in particular, it is often difficult to discern that

---

[2] A richness that generally increases where the supervision session concerns an organisation consulting assignment or a team coaching assignment in which a multitude of people, agendas, projects, ambitions and strategies play a distinct role.

second relationship because they have learned how to shield it carefully. But this doesn't alter the fact that this relationship plays an important role and is inherent to the 'helping' relationship itself. It is a darker, 'shadow' relationship that is unavoidable in 'helping' interactions.

Based on this distribution of roles between supervisee and supervisor, the following patterns can be expected.

- The supervisee submits to supervision by the supervisor in order to learn and develop his own practice. The supervisee is therefore invited to step back and consider his own work from a reflective and critical perspective, and hence to become an observer of his own interventions, assignments and client relationships. But at the same time he is also the protagonist in his work. As the main player in his assignments, he is keen to do them well, ideally to receive reassurance and applause, and preferably to ascribe any tensions to others, not to himself. As an observer, on the other hand, he is keen, together with the supervisor, to take a detached view and apply a critical test of quality to his own work. These two roles (observer and protagonist) always cause friction among themselves, so the supervisee approaches the relationship 'paradoxically' (with internal contradictions) and says: 'help me but please don't be critical', 'change me but without changing me' or 'look at me closely and objectively, but then reassure me'. This is often accompanied by great anxiety – anxiety about what the supervision may trigger or bring to the surface.
- The supervisor starts the relationship on a pedestal: he doesn't have to look at his own problems, issues and practice, but is permitted to do so with respect to the supervisee. However, the role of supervisor also has paradoxical elements, as we saw in Chapter 1. On the one hand, he is keen to preserve his pedestal by radiating expertise, fulfilling his supervisory role and contributing clever ideas or even wisdom. On the other hand, he has to work with largely unfamiliar, 'second-hand' case material. He has to listen and await inspiration, is prone to doubts and to 'not knowing', and he makes mistakes like everyone else. This is also accompanied by great anxiety, anxiety about how and when he 'falls short' as a supervisor.

It is therefore easy to see why even highly experienced coaches and supervisors need reassurance during supervision (Day *et al.* 2008).

A further aggravating factor comes from the biography of people in 'helping' professions (the professions of both supervisee and supervisor). Analysis shows that people often choose a helping profession (partly) in order to handle their own neediness or helplessness better (Miller 1979). By 'nursing' neediness in others, we don't have to feel our own pain while still staying in touch with the 'need for help'. In other words, we can transfer our own need to someone else. This is a basic but, in practice, subtle defence mechanism known as 'projection'. In such circumstances there is also a degree of sublimation of one's own neediness.[3] For the duration of the sessions, we experience

---

[3] For an overview of defence mechanisms such as projection and sublimation, see Chapter 8 of *Coaching with Colleagues* (De Haan and Burger 2005).

what it's like not to need help, to know better, to be a support and anchor for others, and so on. Of all the 'helping professions', this possibility of a 'helper syndrome' is the greatest for supervisors, because choosing that role means that we end up in a 'senior' position and can help not only managers and experts but in fact their helpers as well. At an unconscious level, 'becoming a supervisor' is a sign that we can stop worrying about our own failings and our own neediness, and sit back and enjoy the fact that we have 'made it' and can continue through life as a 'supervisor' or 'untouchable': a fantasy that is of course dispelled by reality. Nevertheless, many supervisors will be very keen to maintain and protect their role and, in particular, not to fail or make mistakes during supervision. In this way, supervisors can continue – without realising it – to nurse their own neediness, to make it bearable, without actually having to confront it.

As a consequence of this role choice and the underlying feelings, supervisor and supervisee will face a huge temptation to organise their mutual reassurance: 'I'll keep you on a pedestal if you don't criticise me too harshly'; 'I'll maintain your ideal picture of an infallible supervisor if you maintain my ideal picture of a functioning consultant'; 'I'll help you look at your assignments from a positive angle, and you'll help me feel good as a supervisor', and so on. This temptation is in fact ever-present, and I have seen the best supervisors succumb to it, fortunately usually on a temporary basis. However, it is important to realise that, if we allow this to happen, as consultants but also as supervisors, we have lost sight of our task and are no longer a supervisor, coach, consultant, or whatever (de Haan 2006). In fact, we are then no more than an addict, in thrall to the quick 'kick' of cheap, positive feedback (Harrison 1997). This giving in to mutual gratification and compliments, to collusion or co-dependence between supervisor and supervisee, or however other authors of different persuasions might term it, would mean the end of the supervision process. Supervision is about taking an independent and frank look at the supervisee's practice, including his failures, shame, doubts and unprocessed or poorly processed experiences.

Occasionally, there is a return to more detached observation and reflection, but it's generally a rough landing. When the spell is broken – i.e. when the supervisor unexpectedly shares a perspective other than the reassuring and flattering one the supervisee is used to – which often happens, understandably, when the supervisor suddenly lets rip with a cynical or arrogant comment (born out of growing irritation because he knows, consciously or unconsciously, that he has strayed away from the supervision task itself), the sparks start to fly and we see an escape into more robust defence mechanisms such as attack, displacement and denial. And there is also an increasing risk of escalation and alienation in the supervision relationship.

It is the job of the supervisor, as the safest, most responsible and objective party in the relationship, to make sure from the outset that they do not yield to these sorts of temptations, and to be open and direct from day one, despite the risk of escalation.[4]

---

[4] The supervisor will find that 'positive transference' – previous experience of 'helping' conversations in a person's life – is on his side here (see also Appendix A). Supervisees generally know from experience, consciously or unconsciously, that this type of candid and uncompromising reflection can also be beneficial and ultimately most useful. Because most consultants and coaches have already had experience as a client of coaching, consulting and/or therapeutic interventions, this factor is generally stronger in supervision than in consulting or coaching.

When the relationship is newly formed that risk is of course much smaller. The supervisee is always well aware that supervision is about learning and that to do that you need to endure unpleasant truths about your own practice. Indeed, the supervisee expects this. And if he doesn't expect it from his supervisor, all the other parties involved in supervision (his own manager, clients, sponsors, professional colleagues, accreditors, etc.) will. In my view, this is why so many executives avoid ever sitting down to work with a coach or consultant and why there are still coaches who manage to avoid ever working with a supervisor. These coaches are well aware that unpleasant or unpalatable things are sometimes said in supervisory relationships, and what could be easier than avoiding them from the very outset?

CASE EXAMPLE

An internal consultant in a corporate environment comes to supervision, with the request to talk about a 'pattern' within her consulting practice as she experiences this at the moment.

As an example, she mentions she is working with a department which is under great pressure to improve bottom-line results. The management team of the department is young and ambitious, has had substantial success in the past, and is now working very hard to demonstrate commercial acumen, rigorous budgeting processes and an ambitious but realistic long-term strategic vision. The board of the company has welcomed the plans but has observed that in their view the present problems – although financial in nature – are not purely to do with top-line growth, finance, operations or strategy. The board thinks they are more to do with people management issues, and they mention motivation and staff turnover as examples. Linda, the internal organisation development consultant, is asked to help the managers of the department through facilitation of their team meetings, engagement of staff, action research, etc.

She has held a three-way meeting with the responsible board member and two preliminary meetings with leaders in the management team. She has left the scheduling of the next steps to her new clients, and she notices that although they occasionally meet in the corridors and then enthusiastically comment that 'we must put something in the diary', in actual fact no action is taken.

Her supervisor explores with her these developments, occasionally halting her in mid-flow as she is bursting into a rich flurry of detail, facts and feelings about the assignment. The supervisor asks questions like, 'Tell me more about your first encounter?', 'How do you feel about this conundrum?' and 'What else is relevant?' Linda is clearly relishing the opportunity to talk this through. She appears very focused and driven.

Then the supervisor thinks he has found something important; could she not just separate the scheduling issues from the actual facilitation and coaching? Could she not just be more proactive in getting the next meetings into the diary? Here he does indeed get close to the nub of the issue for Linda, but not in the way he thinks. Linda believes she cannot do this because it is very central to her assignment that her clients take responsibility for the people management issues. She feels that if she were to be more proactive here, she would establish a relationship where she would carry that responsibility implicitly. So it is important in her view to wait. On the other hand, she herself is impatient to get to grips with this work, precisely because she knows it will ultimately help with the bad state of the department's finances.

The supervisor picks up her sense of urgency and insists, in an obviously helpful yet somehow determined way: 'There are two processes, a diary process and a consulting process. Could you not just separate the two?' At this point a blush and a tear appear on Linda's face, and she is clearly upset about something. The supervisor initially fails to notice as he is pursuing his 'cause', saying, 'Suppose you have two hats on, a "consultant" hat and an "administrator" hat. What would you say with your admin hat on?'

Later, when he does notice Linda's distress, the supervisor tries to calm her by providing more hypotheses about the department she is consulting to, with the opposite effect. Somehow he feels anxious now with the flow of emotions suddenly coming his way. As a result Linda feels completely misunderstood, gets irritated with the supervisor and feels terribly exposed within the session. At that point the supervisor not only realises that he is 'barking up the wrong tree', but also that there is something going on between them in the transference, which contributes to the surge and uncontrollable nature of the emotions on both sides.

Linda is courageous enough to stay with feeling exposed and to explore with the supervisor what might be going on. There is indeed, as Linda mentioned at the very start, a 'pattern'. A pattern of acquiring focus in some areas, yet being unfocused in others; and a pattern of feeling exposed once an authority, like a manager, a consultant or a supervisor, raises the unfocused areas in a rather brusque way. It appears that by not attending to their diaries the management team are making Linda feel not attended to, misunderstood, insufficiently recognised or rewarded for her efforts and ultimately somewhat exposed. They are making her feel how they felt when the feedback from the board came their way. Now, Linda is making her supervisor feel pretty much the same thing. These patterns can lead to a complete breakdown of communication, to feelings of disappointment, irritation, being misunderstood and being inadequate – but fortunately Linda and her supervisor find a way to talk about it so that the profound rupture is significantly healed. Hopefully Linda will in turn feel equipped to talk about these things with her clients.

What we can notice underneath

Another phenomenon that occurs in all relationships, not just 'helping' relationships, is that of projective identification (Klein 1946). This is where the supervisee discovers something of himself in the supervisor and begins unconsciously to identify with it. It is a common relational pattern in people who are under pressure. Under pressure, we sometimes unconsciously and radically simplify our internal and external worlds, in order to rid ourselves of uncertainties and threats that we don't really understand and have little control over. Good and bad are then strictly divided – for example, along the lines of 'work is bad, home is good' or 'boss is bad, but colleagues are good', or 'the rest of the organisation is messing things up, but our department is effective and productive'. Radical caricatures like these make it easier to handle ambivalent and uncontrollable feelings. Exactly the same happens with the internal world – for example, we idealise our own diligence while playing down and brushing aside our tendency to butter people up and try to get into their good books. This tendency towards *splitting* can be seen wherever people are under pressure. The result is feeling better about our own strengths and talents, yet the price we pay is a set of qualities that are kept down and become awkward 'excess baggage'. A solution to that baggage, to those objectionable aspects of ourselves that we are keen to split off and not to examine, is projection. We situate that 'baggage' outside ourselves, and attribute it (unconsciously) to someone else, preferably someone who appears to share the same objectionable aspects. In coaching or supervision, the other person in that setting can serve that purpose. If the other person takes on the projection and behaves accordingly – i.e. accepts the 'baggage' of objectionable aspects and more or less carries it – there is said to be *projective identification* on both sides.[5]

In practice, splitting, projection and projective identification cannot be so clearly differentiated. These phenomena are generally observed more as an interaction in which two (or more) parties develop a skewed relationship. This doesn't alter the fact that the end situation, shared projective identification – a complementary process between two individuals who split off, project, and identify with parts of each other – is clearly recognisable in many relationships, particularly longstanding relationships. Projective identification can therefore occur in a variety of relationships, and particularly so in helping, caring, consulting relationships, including supervision. Because projective identification is a complex process that can be understood from many perspectives, we will discuss two detailed examples. We start with an example that illustrates the sharp edges of the phenomenon, first in the splitting of good and bad aspects and then in the aggression towards the target of projection (the supervisor). The typical way in which the supervisor feels driven into a corner is recognisable in both examples. The only way the supervisor can get out of it is by bringing up the process itself, but there is a strong chance that he will be regarded by the supervisee as a 'persecutor' or 'accuser' (Klein 1946).

CASE EXAMPLE

On the surface this member of a supervision group had been very engaged and collaborative, but one always felt there was something brewing underneath. As well as pleasant, friendly and enthused, she also appeared somewhat aloof, competitive and ill at ease. She appeared much more lively in the breaks than in the sessions themselves. At the beginning of this group meeting it was agreed that she would coach one other member of the group. When the time for that session came, after the break, she appeared not to remember the agreement and brought some client work of her own – in fact, the same

---

[5] For the idea of mutual projective identification, Bion (1962) introduced the terms 'container' and 'contained'.

client she had already brought to the previous session. When the group reminded her of this, she instantly changed to another client. The supervisor reminded everyone of the initial agreement, but as the colleague she was about to work with did not mind doing a swap, the supervisor allowed the pair to carry on in reversed roles.

The client that was brought was described as 'weird', someone who behaves erratically, is often frustrated, and sends around group emails – for example, recently to all colleagues about his experiences on a course. The client also had an ambition to change the whole way his office operates which would be well out of proportion to his formal remit and responsibility.

The coach and supervisee discussed the case with the help of the group consultation method (see Chapter 6), at the end of which various members of the group offered their comments and feedback. The supervisor waited until everyone had spoken and then made a link between the 'weird' client and the 'weird' beginning of the supervision session itself. This made the supervisee initially quite defensive: she explained herself, argued that the original agreement had been for her to bring client work, etc. The supervisor continued interpreting and made a link with motivation, suggesting that the supervisee may have been ambivalent in terms of her motivation and preparedness to take supervision seriously. The next day the supervisor received an email in which the supervisee asked for a 'quick chat' about the session, suggesting that there were a few things going on, including parallel processes, that the supervisor might find worthwhile exploring.

Here we have a typical example of the vulnerable areas of the supervisee being projected into the supervisor: initially, during the session, confusion, ambivalence and an inability to read situations (both the format of the session and the situation of the 'weird' client). Not only are these projected into the supervisor, they are then also quite strongly attacked. The supervisor is being nudged into giving up time outside the session, discussing the case further, and even learning from the case as one would expect the supervisee to be doing. In terms of communication and roles the supervisee becomes the supervisor and employs the language of the supervisor. During the phone call the supervisee says she was struck most by a 'parallel process between us' as she had noticed the supervisor had (in her view) become quite emotional at the end of the session, perhaps unable to handle the case.

Other than as a reversal of the supervisory relationship, everything that the supervisee says at this stage can be understood as being directed to that vulnerable, exposed part of herself that she is presently not acknowledging (and that she has unconsciously located within the supervisor). As this was only a limited contract (and on the phone we are now well outside the boundaries of formal supervision), the supervisor decided to respond gently and affirmatively, noticing how the supervisory relationship had deepened and the two of them were now closer than before in the sessions. Raising the projective-identification process that is felt to be going on would be a far too challenging intervention for this supervisee at this time.

The next example of projective identification, this time at the start of the supervision relationship, comes from the book *Dynamisch begeleiden* by van Gorkum (2007: 27).

Here, we see the supervisor not avoiding the role of 'persecutor' but actually bringing up the unpalatable dynamic. This tactic leads to a breakthrough.

CASE EXAMPLE

We had had our first session and were supposed to discuss the supervisee's learning objectives in the second session. On being asked what he wanted to learn from this supervision, the supervisee launched into a detailed account of his work. Although I interrupted him many times, because he was only telling me what he did and how well it was going for him and I wasn't hearing anything about his learning objectives and issues, I didn't manage to get an answer to my question. I still remember the thoughts and feelings that surfaced in me during that session. They were feelings of irritation, boredom, anger, indifference and powerlessness, and thoughts such as: 'How do I get rid of this guy?' and 'Okay, I'll just wait it out.'

Towards the end of the session, he fell silent and I said to him: 'You've been speaking for over an hour. I tried to intervene, unsuccessfully. I was angry. I was bored and I felt powerless, because everything's going well for you. What I've been wondering the whole time is what you want from me as a supervisor.'

He was silent for a minute or two before stammering out the following answer: 'I want you to he-he-he-he-he-help me.'

Looking at this example from the supervisee's perspective, we can see that, by monopolising the conversation and not heeding my question, he adopts a closed-off and impervious attitude. In so doing he delegates to me, as the supervisor, the role of maintaining the contact and connection. I am therefore assigned the role of approaching him, which I do several times, but in vain. As a result, the supervisee doesn't have to fear ending up in the risky territory of neediness, his forbidden area. That this is his prohibited area is clear to me from the stammering answer that he finally gives. The projective identification can take place by putting me in a position of neediness. My reactions show that I am not keen to be put in that position. I become angry, irritated, indifferent and bored. These are feelings that I do evidently allow myself, because I experience them quite consciously. The feelings of powerlessness and neediness are more remote for me. You don't like to be helpless as a supervisor, and certainly not in a second session.

In conclusion we can say that projective identification, although a very common defence mechanism in helping relationships, is very difficult for the supervisor to handle. This is due to the primitive nature of splitting and projection, an origin which is remote from reflection and verbal processing. Moreover, there is a real risk of a projective identification reaction on the part of the supervisor. Splitting and projection foster splitting and projection in the other person, with the risk that the supervisor will join in the game, so to speak, and no longer have his hands free for reflection. If the supervisor manages not to do this and is able to maintain his own 'helping' role, it is still risky to reflect on what is taking place here and now, in other words to bring up the subject of projective identification itself. The supervisor is usually seen as a persecutor when he does come around to bringing it up. What the supervisor says will be received in terms of projective identification. The supervisor is immediately seen as that (unconsciously projected) 'bad', 'dysfunctional' or 'weak' part of the supervisee himself that is only out to disparage the supervisee or to confront him with his own shortcomings. The tactic of naming projective identification can succeed only if it is backed up by clear examples, and is used within a safe setting. A good starting point is generally the ambivalence that is inherent in all projective identification. The supervisor links to the roots of splitting and also shows empathy for ambivalent feelings, which have a right to exist in themselves in terms of, for example, an unsatisfactory dilemma, a painful situation or a difficult decision.

Incidentally, I have found that it is indeed possible to bring up projective identification and thereby overcome it, but this can take some time. It often starts with a single observation, as in the case example given above, which is experienced as hurtful or provocative. Then it is necessary to name that reaction – that second development in the relationship – to enable the full picture to be mapped out. For example, a supervisor might say: 'I feel as if you leave the initiative to me during our sessions, and as if you are somehow expecting that I am the one to learn from our sessions and that this has little to do with you or your practice. When I bring that up, you react with irritation and start to explain to me how important the supervision is to you, how much you've learned from supervision, and what you've done with supervision – but my feeling persists. That leaves me only two choices: either keep working away myself while still feeling that it's not really getting through to you, or say something about it and end up in a war of words. I think we've come to an impasse with these two options, and there won't be any learning as long as we continue to work like this.'

Using empathy

We have presented an outline of observations and phenomena that can be brought to the surface by listening closely to (supervision) relationships. To keep it simple, we used a framework that shifts the focus of listening between:

1   The content of the case material.
2   The supervisory relationship itself, or the level of interaction.
3   Our own emotions.
4   Our own distraction.

If we shift the focus of our attention as consciously and truthfully as possible we will, in my view, automatically develop empathy for what is being brought to the supervision from moment to moment.

The topic of 'empathic listening' can also be approached differently, with an equally useful framework that overlaps with the previous one. In this case we describe listening as a sequence of: (1) understanding and getting a feel for the case material, to (2) getting a deeper feel for what is going on in ourselves as we listen to the case material, to (3) getting a deeper feel for what is going on in the other person – the supervisee – as he talks to us, to (4) getting a deeper feel for what must be going on in the other person's client at this moment or in the situation described. What we do then is develop a personal rapport with respectively (1) the case material, (2) our own listening self, (3) the supervisee and (4) the supervisee's client.

In other words, the technique we are using here – and especially in steps 3 and 4 – is one that was long ago described as *trial identification* (by Fliess in 1942; see also Casement 2002). Trial identification is an attempt to get an idea of how this relationship feels here and now for the other person – i.e. how the supervisee might experience the supervisor at this moment in time. It is a trial or experiment in identifying with the other person – hence the term. Trial identification is a good way of assessing the extent to which one's own impressions about the relationship may or may not exist in the other person. Moreover, trial identification explores how certain things that we ourselves have said as supervisors might come across to the other person. During a trial identification we attempt as best we can to conduct a test or trial of the way this relationship feels, here and now, for the other person.

In supervision, this technique of trial identification can be extended to the other person's client or clients – i.e. to the people involved in the assignment the supervisee is currently discussing. How do they experience the relationship with their consultant or coach at this moment in time? How would they assess what the supervisee and supervisor are cooking up at this moment? Particularly where suggestions or interpretations are put forward by the supervisor, trial identification with the client is a good measure of the usefulness or feasibility of those suggestions. It is not an easy technique, because it requires us to make a genuine attempt to observe the world and ourselves through the eyes of our supervisee – or even through the eyes of the latter's client. It is therefore a highly critical and, especially, self-critical experiment that, provided it is entered into fearlessly, yields real rewards. The trial generates ways of seeing one's own feelings, thoughts, judgements and conclusions in a new light. According to Casement, we can develop trial identification into a form of 'internal supervision' – i.e. a form of supervision of ourselves as we work with clients and supervisees. He gives many examples of trial identification in his book *Learning from our Mistakes* (2002).

What the frameworks described above have in common is a shifting of the listener between different positions: himself, the material, the supervisee, the client, the relationship now, the supervisee–client relationship, etc. Another well-known model which opens up a similar array of perspectives on the same session is Hawkins and Shohet's (2006) seven-eyed supervision model, which distinguishes seven 'eyes' or 'modes': the client; the coaching/consulting interventions; the client–supervisee relationship; the supervisee; the supervisee–supervisor relationship; the supervisor; and the wider context. Listening under the surface therefore means never being satisfied with your current impressions, never resting on your laurels, always striking out upon new paths in order to view the emerging 'material' differently, always making fresh attempts to get a feel for and empathise with the other person. Such listening forms the basis of good supervision; indeed, such listening makes up the bulk of the supervisor's work. I am firmly of the opinion that 90 per cent of the techniques of a good supervisor are in fact listening or empathetic techniques. What is more, the other techniques follow of their own accord – i.e., 99 per cent of the actual work of supervision is in listening.

An overview of parallel processes

In the previous section we discussed a number of well-known phenomena in supervision relationships, such as resistance to change, the helper syndrome and projective identification. In this section we will look at a number of phenomena which concern the influence of one relationship upon another, or the way in which the forming of one relationship is governed to some extent by other relationships. These are *transference phenomena* or *parallel processes*.

Thus far, we have seen how the results of supervision are largely achieved both by considering the case material and endowing it with new meaning, and by considering the supervision session itself and endowing it with meaning. Meaning is not something magical that just appears out of the blue; it has to be understood as a process: a process of ongoing listening and ongoing linking to information that comes from the four layers of observation: content, interaction, own emotion and own distraction. Meaning is rarely experienced as new. Occasionally, meaning is experienced as a different perspective or as something that the supervisee does know but hasn't considered, accepted or taken on board. The activity of supervision, via listening and the assigning of meaning, generates patterns that are meaningful in themselves and that contain much of the value of supervision. It is therefore worth listening closely to the supervision process itself. To this end, it is useful to map out the multiple layers and parallel processes, albeit with the warning that a map is different from the terrain itself, and that the actual results of supervision lie in unique, personal sense-making processes and not in abstract labels, jargon or constructs.

In this section we discuss the following patterns: ordinary parallel, reverse parallel, organisation parallel and classical transference. Which of these patterns is chosen during the supervision session seems to depend largely on the relational resonance or valencies (Bion 1961) of supervisee and supervisor (see Chapter 4). In principle, any of these patterns can be used to express a parallel process (Sumerel 1994). In supervision I often devote time to making these patterns explicit in a bid to learn from transference phenomena. As far as I have been able to ascertain, Harold Searles (1955) was the first person to use the term 'parallel process' and he also distinguished two forms of parallel processes. His terms are therefore are given in brackets.

Ordinary parallel (Searles' unconscious identification)

This is the phenomenon whereby a supervision session starts to resemble the coaching or consulting session, this time with the supervisee in the role of client. A congruent parallel process of this kind has a purpose that is perhaps a combination of the following mechanisms.

- *Transfer of information*: the supervisee shows by his actions how the client comes across and what, for example, is difficult about his client's behaviour.

- *Acting out*: the supervisee retaliates, so to speak, against the client who has given him such a difficult time in the consulting session by adopting that difficult behaviour himself. As a result, he himself can reap the benefits promised by such behaviour in a session.
- *Spontanous learning behaviour*: the supervisee explores his client's behaviour, in a sense, by adopting it himself.[6] He attempts an understanding of his client by role-playing and experiencing the client's behaviour, with the qualification that this understanding remains largely implicit and unconscious and that it takes a clever supervisor to alert the supervisee to these learning benefits. Chapter 1 gave an example of a coach who, during supervision, started to resemble the exuberant Italian client who had been causing him trouble.

Reverse parallel (Searles' complementary unconscious identification)

Here, the supervisee keeps the same role in the session as he had in the original coaching or consulting session, while the supervisor starts unconsciously to assume patterns of behaviour displayed by the client in the coaching or consulting relationship. This can be very difficult for the supervisee, because the supervision starts to feel just as frustrating as the session under discussion. The supervision session appears not to help, in fact the conversation seems only to make it worse for the supervisee. The supervisee needs courage to break out of the pattern. While this requires a special talent on the part of the supervisor because the conversation feels much less frustrating for him, he is often the only one to sense that there is something wrong, by observing the supervisee closely. This reverse parallel presentation seems less promising at the outset: all the supervisee is doing is repeating himself. On the other hand, an interpretation that draws the supervisee's behaviour to his attention is often very productive: the supervisee suddenly discovers how, and to what extent, he himself is contributing to a degree of 'stuckness' or misunderstanding in his own client relationship.

Organisation parallel

This is a phenomenon whereby a 'detail' of the consulting finds its way into the supervision and starts to play a leading role. These details are often cultural or behavioural aspects of the organisation with which the supervisee is closely connected – in other words, cultural aspects that have infected the consultant and are unconsciously magnified in the supervision session. It is often thanks to such parallels from the client organisation that we discover anything new at all; new in the sense that it was not known or intuited by the supervisee about that organisation. After all, direct impressions from within the organisation are not available and documents offer only facts which may be utterly irrelevant to the supervisee–client work. An example of this comes from a coach working for a high-tech company in a fast-moving market where managers can expect to be given a new role or job description every three months on average. The coach is

---

[6] This is an example of unconscious trial identification (Fliess 1942).

very matter-of-fact about it all, displaying a resignation that is in fact a reflection of the resignation that prevails in the high-tech company itself. The supervisor, who doesn't have assignments in that organisation and to whom such a culture is a novelty, can cast doubts on that resignation itself. He can interpret it as a form of acquiescence with respect to the decisions of senior management in that organisation. This may open up a new field of investigation around the question of whether it is possible for managers to have an impact, to achieve success, when they are only put in post for months rather than years.

Classical transference

Similarities may develop in the supervisory relationship between one or more of the supervisee's previous relationships and this session now. In this case there is not so much a parallel process with the supervisee's clients, as with other significant relationships of the supervisee. This occurs mainly with the supervisor in the role of that other, earlier relationship (and so in reverse parallel form). Not infrequently, the patterns that emerge appear on further inspection to be relevant to the supervisee's client(s) as well. An obvious example of this phenomenon is the older supervisor who comes across to the supervisee (unconsciously) as a 'mother figure' or 'father figure' and with whom the supervisee therefore – without realising it – enters into the same 'juvenile' or 'infantile' relationship that was so defining in his own life.

All parallel processes, just like projective identification, develop unconsciously in the first instance. As supervisors, we don't discover them until we feel that 'something' is going on, without knowing what. We may feel, for example, that we are starting to get bogged down (frustration, in layer 3: our own emotions), or that we are straying away from the case material in some other way (boredom, in layer 4: distraction). All transference phenomena share the feature that, at an unconscious level, a relationship is forced upon both participants, a relationship that is not (entirely) in keeping with the supervisor–supervisee relationship and that comes from somewhere else, such as the consulting work that the supervisor and supervisee are discussing.

It is the supervisor's task to listen attentively and thereby identify this enforced relationship and bring it up for discussion in one way or another. However, he doesn't always manage to do so of course. If it isn't identified – i.e. if a relationship is forced upon us and we are not (consciously) aware of it – we can respond in one of two ways: *symmetrically*, by 'fighting back' in order to fend off the enforced role and thus implicitly transfer it back to our supervisee, or *complementarily* by unconsciously accepting and even embracing the role and so implicitly joining in the game with the supervisee. We can recognise a symmetrical reaction in ourselves because we get active, frustrated or irritated in this relationship. We can recognise a complementary reaction because we wander astray, become distracted from the task at hand and hence from the case material, and sometimes because we feel flattered and, so to speak, start to feel *too* comfortable in this relationship. Symmetrical supervision relationships tend towards escalation, conflict and friction, while complementary supervision relationships tend towards boredom, superficiality and detachment.

CASE EXAMPLE: PARALLEL PROCESSES

A supervisee starts to talk about a recent coaching session, his eighth session with a board member of a high-tech organisation. His client had talked about the introduction of a new IT system, with speeches about the future of the industry and simulations for users of the system. The client was pleased with how the day had gone.

Any supervision session can become dominated by a parallel process which may recreate the client session or the thrust of all eight client sessions and can therefore provide a valuable window into those client sessions. Here are five possible outcomes:

1 Ordinary parallel: the supervisor feels similarly superfluous and is somewhat intimidated by the way in which his supervisee goes through the material and the way in which he doesn't appear to expect any input from the supervisor.

2 Reverse parallel: the supervisor starts to explain to the supervisee what he might do with this client and how he can challenge his client more.

3 Organisation parallel: the transience of the case and the lightness of tone of the supervisee spread to the supervisor, who starts to approach the situation with a businesslike acumen and who switches to a different topic after a couple of feeble summaries. In fact, transience and superficiality are some of the problems that this organisation has, but that fact goes unnoticed in the supervision.

4 Classical transference: the supervisee's complaining tone grows ever stronger; in the session he becomes less and less contented with himself and his own actions, and discontented with the supervisor as well (although that isn't said). The supervisee learned this form of counter-dependence or 'passive aggression' early on, in his relationship with his parents.

5 Projective identification: the supervisee is not comfortable with his own anxiety or awe around this client and therefore poses as self-assured during supervision. The supervisor starts to feel intimidated and anxious and also inhibited in terms of his own interventions. In the end, he is able to put into words how the supervisee may also feel inhibited in this high-tech environment. And possibly his client, the board member in the organisation, feels the same. This leads to a breakthrough.

The fascinating thing about parallel processes is that the supervisor *has* to get involved and finds that his own ideal or the illusion of a distant, 'wise' supervisor is thoroughly shattered. The central role and direct involvement of the supervisor himself, the fact that he himself, however briefly, is now part of the problem and himself is maintaining something that is holding up the supervision, results in conscious identification or acknowledgment of parallel processes that is generally very liberating. Moreover, as a result of putting a name to parallel processes, changes often occur automatically in the case material and the supervisee feels that he has really been helped.

Here is another overview of these slightly overlapping terms referring to unconscious processes:

1   *Transference* is the phenomenon where the supervisee 'transfers' past experiences onto this supervisory relationship so that it looks or feels the same as 'back then'.
2   *Counter-transference* is the same, but this time the supervisor 'transfers' past experiences onto this supervisory relationship so that it looks or feels the same as 'back then' for him.
3   *Parallel process* is when past patterns are recreated by *both* partners, as it were 'intersubjectively' – i.e. between or among the conversational partners.

When we have these phenomena at play in supervision, something shifts and changes in the field or conversational space between supervisor and supervisee, in a variety of ways:

1   When a new pattern is introduced in the field between supervisor and supervisee, this pattern may in part originate from emotive and significant experiences outside of the room, but may also in part originate from the meeting itself and its significance for the participants. So either the supervisee may have been triggered to transfer by highly emotive or impactful client work experiences, or may just as well have been triggered by the anxiety of being in supervision or being with this particular supervisor, or by both. Alternatively, the pattern may have been triggered by the supervisor responding to something in the client material recounted. Usually, all these different 'causes' of transference have some truth in them and the pattern will only really establish itself if there is 'multi-causality': influences from many sides.
2   We may find ourselves part of an *ordinary parallel* re-creation, where the earlier relationship is re-created with the supervisee in two different roles – in other words, where the supervisee somehow does to the supervisor what the client did to him; or rather a *reverse parallel* recreation, where the supervisee keeps the role he had in the other, earlier relationship – in other words, where the supervisee re-enacts how he was in the session with the client.
3   If the supervisee transfers certain patterns, the supervisor as the other person in the room has three choices: (a) to go along and co-create a parallel process; (b) to move against and impose other patterns; or (c) to observe and reflect on what is happening here and now. As transferential processes are unconscious, the third option is once-removed as compared to the others, and hence more difficult to embark on.
4   If supervisee and supervisor move to the option (c) above, that of reflecting on patterns, they start using their counter-transference as a creative source for understanding this conversation and the work of the supervisee. They can hypothesise whether what they notice has a bearing on the client organisation, the client's relationships, the client–supervisee relationship specifically, other client work of the supervisee, other client work of the supervisor, etc. For this it is important to ask the question: 'What has triggered me to become part of this pattern?', or 'What do we think has prompted this change in the relational field between us?'

Transference processes are often influenced by *projective processes*, where some present feeling or self-experience is split off and projected into the other person. As this also happens unconsciously and without mention in conversation, it may also trigger an unconscious response, either projecting back or triggering transferential patterns. Splitting and projection may easily lead to the phenomenon of projective identification, where there is an appeal to the other person to *identify* with what was split off. Projective identification, although not transferential in origin, can lead to very similar changes in the relational field which are worth asking questions about. And it can lead to very similar responses from the other person, in terms of going along, moving against, or (hopefully, in supervision) observing and reflecting upon.

For those readers who want to explore the concepts of transference and parallel processes in more depth, Appendix A has a historical account of their discovery and application.

Fearlessness put to the test

What sort of picture are we now starting to get of supervision and the techniques of the supervisor? On the one hand, supervision seems to mean oscillating to and fro between a variety of relationship patterns. Moreover, the case material brought in by supervisees tends to consist of some of the most complex, multi-layered, ethically problematic and politically sensitive assignments they are involved in at that moment in time. It's not without reason that the supervisee chooses this specific case material in preference to all other. We can therefore imagine the supervisor as both at the mercy of the conversation and as a beacon of reflection floating on a sea of complexity. On the other hand, we *can* often assume that a positive basic relationship will quickly develop between supervisee and supervisor, with a sufficient degree of trust in the available help and reflection. A good working alliance (Greenson 1965) is often easier to build in supervision than in coaching or consulting. The supervisees themselves have also been exposed to difficult professional conversations. So they know what it is to struggle and grope one's way through such conversations as one tries to help clients deal with the issues facing them. The task of supervision may be complex and confusing, but the basic relationship is generally good.

Supervision sessions inevitably have an element of 'confession' about them. A consultant with a busy practice has a session with his supervisor, say, once a month. He has had a variety of conversations with clients and colleagues, has written reports and proposals and played a leading role in work conferences, meetings or development programmes. No doubt he has experienced a range of issues, doubts, successes and surprises in the course of this work. The unspoken, psychological contract of supervision appears implicitly to say the following: 'From that variety of conversations and interventions, select the one you had most doubts about and that makes you feel the worst. We will discuss that particular event and look at what you could have done differently, so that you don't come across the same problems again next month.'

It is certainly useful for the supervisee to talk about those client and working relationships that present him with the most questions and doubts. In general, in a good supervision relationship, you can start almost anywhere and within a short space of time you will come across doubts, dilemmas and uncertainties 'as a matter of course'.

This means that something of the confessional, a sort of ongoing admission of the sins and shame of the consultant or coach, cannot be denied in supervision. Indeed, without the pain of mistakes made, without frustration at the realisation that it is now in many ways too late, without frustration over recurring sensitivities that keep cropping up and without feelings of envy (of the supervisor among others, who never has to confess anything), it probably wouldn't work. Reason enough for even the best, those that are keenest to learn, to develop defences against supervision. Reason enough not to be surprised at the accounts by supervisees saying they specifically do not bring their most shameful or painful experiences to supervision and avoid exposing themselves to such sensitivities (Gray *et al.* 2001), partly to avoid their own pain and doubts, partly to spare the supervisor and not to saddle him with painful or shameful events. Reason enough also to expect some degree of hope for forgiveness, absolution or penitence either from the supervisor or from the supervisee himself.

It is good to bear in mind in this connection that the Christian tradition has also placed a huge emphasis on (self-)confession. Christianity understands confessions in terms of owning up to sins, which involves a penance. That basic principle is less productive in supervision in my opinion because it assumes an asymmetry between supervisor and supervisee and puts pressure on confessions. A pressure that will take two forms: pressure towards the act of confessing itself and pressure to view what you are confessing as bad, sinful or impure.

Foucault (1982) shows how confessions can also be interpreted quite differently, namely as a sincere self-examination. He outlines a tradition that runs from Pythagoras to statesman-philosophers such as Seneca and Marcus Aurelius, in which confessions, in the form of self-examination or meditation, have much more to do with 'purifying the conscience', 'checking the stocks', 'inspecting the day-by-day activities', or 'withdrawing into contemplation after the pressures of work'. This is much more in the spirit of modern supervision, although it is useful to bear in mind that your partner in supervision (be it supervisor or supervisee) may be more influenced by the idea of confession and penance. This may inhibit them from working with confessions openly and constructively.

This 'confessional' aspect is one reason why the supervisor's frankness is put to the test. On the one hand, it seems important to develop a warm, respectful and safe relationship in which shameful things can be said; on the other hand, the objective remains to actively open up areas of shame, to continue to observe patterns and to help face defences fearlessly.

CASE EXAMPLE

A consultant sees a particular chief executive once a week, on a Wednesday, and receives weekly supervision himself. He has therefore committed to keeping all of his Wednesdays free, except outside term times, and to be available on the agreed hour for his once-weekly client. But he also does other consulting work which sometimes encroaches upon his Wednesdays. As a result, he is now facing a month in which he has to move his client to a Tuesday on two occasions, an action that he himself knows will be difficult for this vulnerable client. He is likely to feel rejected, and may as a consequence cancel appointments himself as a form of retaliation. This wouldn't benefit the ongoing work, where they are only gradually taking tiny steps forward. With his supervisor, the consultant discusses the action to be taken.

When the supervisor says something about the emotions the consultant is going to bring down on himself, he responds with slight irritation and tries to play down the situation, along the lines of, 'Moving from a Wednesday to a Tuesday isn't the end of the world . . .'. The supervisor stays with that irritation, despite the fact that his client would clearly prefer to talk about something else. What's more, he comes back to it in the next two supervision sessions. In those sessions, he describes the irritation as self-importance and says: 'Why does your client mind these reschedulings so much? Well, partly because you just assume for the sake of convenience that he will fit in with your schedule. It comes as no surprise to me that he should start to feel manipulated.'

And indeed, the client cancelled twice in the same month, once on a Tuesday and once on a Wednesday.

Where a supervisee shares confessions candidly with a supervisor, it can be difficult for the latter to confront him with critical observations and comments without succumbing to a tendency to come across as a smart-ass or in some way superior in the conversation. Criticism can be given *ex cathedra*, inspired by the supervisor's superiority and a dogmatic way of thinking. In giving such criticism, the supervisor runs the risk of undermining and weakening the working alliance that is so important for supervision. For me, it sometimes feels as if I'm attempting to speak through a raging storm, a storm of objections, wounds, sensitivities, shame and self-criticism, that could easily lift me off the ground and send me flying. But despite that storm and those persistent showers, the wet snow blowing in my face, I still have to speak and acknowledge my modest truth – if only because I know that that small truth, that conviction I hold at this very moment about what I am observing, that inspiration that strikes me without much idea of where it comes from, constitutes the essence of my work as a supervisor. If, for reasons of hygiene, self-protection, indecision, timidity, sympathy, fear or indeed anything else, I fail to honour my small truth and explore whether that small kernel of truth (often derived from a flash of inspiration, a maverick idea, a spontaneous question) might grow into a larger truth concerning the client or my supervisee, I abandon the arena of supervision and am no longer worth my fee as a supervisor.

Fearless supervision, which echoes the term 'fearless compassion' in Hawkins and Smith (2006), is also made more difficult by the other roles that a supervisor has. As underlined in Chapter 1, within the scope of the case material and the supervision sessions we have the responsibilities of developer, gatekeeper and nurse all at the same time. So far in this chapter I have spoken mainly about the developing role which involves supervisors endeavouring to feed observations back to their supervisees. But in the role of gatekeeper, critical observations in particular carry a different charge: the supervisee may easily believe the supervisor is expressing disapproval or a negative opinion with regard to the supervisee's practice. It is therefore important, when feeding back observations, to make it clear that certain comments, including the critical ones, are intended to support learning. In most supervision relationships this is self-evident because the gatekeeper role is either less prominent or is more formally regulated in a written document drawn up once a year.

The role of nurse sometimes obliges us to eschew developing interventions completely because we have to focus on the supervisee's overall condition and look more at his handling of stress, balance, work boundaries and working conditions. This is not very common either, but it is important again to define a clear and explicit boundary between the different roles.

By way of a summary, here is a brief list of reasons why 'fearless speech', the relentless and overt observation of the case material, however necessary it may be in supervision, is often under pressure.

- The case material and the helping relationship are complex and sometimes internally contradictory, so we never know for certain what we're observing and what we're missing at the same time.
- We are seeking not a consulting but a reflective role: the supervisee knows more than we do about the material and holds full responsibility for his own client relationships.
- As a supervisor, we feel we are part of parallel processes and hence never know for certain if we've got the wrong end of the stick or if our counter-transference is suggesting something to us.
- Due to the confessional nature of supervision, it feels cruel to come up with a cutting observation.
- Feeding back frank observations is not the same as confronting on the basis of our other roles, those of gatekeeper and nurse, so we always have to find the right tone and make it clear that we are not expressing disapproval or concern when we are merely feeding back observations fearlessly.

My book on fearless consulting (de Haan 2006) contains more on the art of frank and fearless speech, why it is so important for consultants (and supervisors), and how it often comes under pressure.

Summary

The supervisor's most important technique is that of observing, listening and recording what is brought into the session on various levels.

1. Content of case material:
   a facts relating to the case;
   b supervisee's emotions while giving his account;
   c supervisee's intentions while giving his account;
   d metaphors, stammering, slips of the tongue, choice of words and other use of language;
   e gestures and other non-verbal signals.
2. Level of interaction:
   a The helping relationship *above the surface*: working alliance or 'positive transference':
      * agreement on objectives;
      * agreement on tasks;
      * bond or emotional attachment.
   b The helping relationship *under the surface*:
      * division of roles between supervisor and supervisee;
      * projective identification.
   c Reflections of other relationships (transference phenomena):
      * ordinary parallel;
      * reverse parallel;
      * organisation parallel;
      * classical transference.
3. Own emotions or discoveries:
   a doubt/anxiety versus certainty/conviction;
   b positive emotions such as love, joy and surprise;
   c negative emotions such as anger, sadness and fear.
4. Outside the case material and the setting, by 'being distracted':
   a the personal agenda finding its way into the supervision situation;
   b being distracted as a safety valve on one's own suppressed emotions.

This process of observation can be coupled with *trial identification*: observing from the other's point of view.

The art of supervision is:
* to capture as much as possible within all of these layers and more;
* to identify patterns of phenomena that are expressed on one level, but are more connected with another level

and requires
* a large measure of *fearlessness* in feeding back all of these observations.

3 Techniques of the supervisee: scales of reflection

SUPERVISION AS...
A beacon of reflection floating in a sea of complexity

In many ways it is much more difficult to be a supervisee than a supervisor. Exposing your practice to supervision means discussing all your doubts, hesitations, emotions and spontaneous discoveries with your supervisor. That alone is no easy task. On top of that, you are then expected to reflect further on all of those things. In the process, you soon discover more doubts, tensions and unpalatable revelations. And you also discover the limits of your own reflections. You notice how you block your own reflections and indeed how in some cases you preclude generating any breakthroughs or insights. All of these characteristics of supervision are painful but nonetheless important, if only to get to know yourself better and to steel yourself to embrace the challenges of your practice. It helps, therefore, to hone your ability to handle supervision: the quality of the supervisee's techniques is at least as important for the success of supervision as the technical input of the supervisor.[1] Supervisee techniques are first and foremost reflective techniques and techniques for controlling emotions. The supervisor can of course help and lend support.

Reflection-action-reflection and reflection-in-action

In supervision you commit yourself to reflecting on your consulting or coaching practice. There are two ways in which reflection makes you a better coach and consultant. One is that by reflection you improve your own potential action and enhance your practice. The other is that by reflection on your reflection (meta-reflection) you learn how to strengthen your clients' reflection processes.

Reflecting, like relating, is both direct object and verb in the sentence that starts with supervision. 'You are in supervision to reflect on your reflection process', and equally, 'You are in supervision to enter into a relationship that puts your relationships under the microscope'. Reflection, like relation, is a key activity in supervision, in which you attempt to improve by engaging in reflection and receiving feedback from your supervisor. This can only be beneficial for your own consulting and coaching assignments.[2]

Of these two (relationships and reflections), it is hard to say which is more fundamental: relationships are improved by reflection. But the opposite is also true; reflection is improved considerably by staying in touch with another person who participates in your reflection. This chapter starts with a brief introduction to reflection. It then goes on to discuss some suggestions as to how reflection can be brought closer to action and relationship.

Much has already been written about various forms of reflection after action (Garvin 2000), reflection in action (Kolb 1984), reflection on reflection in action (Schön 1983) and reflection before action (Cunningham 1994). Essentially we re-learn in every supervisory relationship to separate reflection from action (i.e. to organise it separately from the consulting assignments) and at the same time to bring the fruits of reflection back to action. We learn to design and go through a reflection-action cycle. This means opening up recollections of action and experience (consulting sessions) to further processing, and bringing the conclusions of that processing back to the practical setting of the consulting sessions.

But we also learn to separate reflection from passivity (i.e. to organise it separately from the supervision) and at the same time to bring the fruits of that action back to reflection. We learn to create reflection-in-action moments. In other words, we learn to

---

[1] So it's a good thing that Carroll and Gilbert have already written an entire book for the supervisee (2005).

[2] There is some empirical evidence from modern attachment research that reflection can be a powerful and useful mental activity: for example, Fonagy *et al.* (1994) demonstrate with a group of relatively high-stress single-parent families that they have a much higher chance of securely attached infants if their capacity to reflect on mental states (mentalisation), operationalised by reflective-self function, is higher. There is now a whole literature on the benefits of 'mentalisation' – the capacity to understand and reflect on one's own and others' mental states.

take the reflective attitude that developed during supervision with us to our practice, and so to do our actual work with greater focus and reflection.

Reflection-action cycles and reflection-in-action moments are two sides of the same coin, just as in relationships the two individuals and the relationship they have created together (the 'in-between', the process) also represent two sides of the same coin. Indeed, reflection *is* relation and relation *is* reflection. Take a look at the original meanings of these words. Reflection originally meant 'bending back' (Latin *reflectere*), while relation means 'bringing back' (Latin *relatus*, from *referre*), a very similar concept.

What do you do as a supervisee in order to reflect?

1   In the first place, step outside of the slumber and comfort zone where we all spend the vast majority of our waking hours. Break out of the endless repetition of non-reflective thoughts – i.e. really wake up.[3]
2   Relate accounts of your practice, embellished with facts and feelings, as they occur to you here and now.
3   Play with those accounts, reorder and restructure them, but also embellish them and think up possible new endings based on the same material.
4   Look critically at those facts and accounts, at your own actions and those of your clients, at the consequences of those actions, and also at the metaphors and 'sources' of the accounts, in your own life but also in the organisations and lives of your clients.
5   Listen to other ways of seeing: interruptions, interpretations and new, incompatible accounts given by the supervisor.
6   Admit and acknowledge that you sometimes get stuck, that you have doubts, that you are puzzled, or that you don't have an account, solution or answer to offer.
7   Choose the consequences of new insights and be prepared to allow your practice to change accordingly, with progressive insight.

CASE EXAMPLE

In a group supervision session with John, he talks about a client whom he has seen for three sessions. His client seems to have difficulty committing to the sessions. Frequently, he seems to be engaging in 'social chat' rather than using the sessions for his benefit. He rarely brings specific issues even though as far as John can tell there are bound to be many. Also, he seems to be expressing a wish for certain interventions and not others, in particular for 'teaching' interventions where he wants to draw directly on John's experience, and for 'affirming' interventions where he seems to want reassurance from John. John obviously wants to do well for his client, but struggles to choose an approach or to stay with it.

---

[3] Having given the etymology of reflections and relationships, it is perhaps relevant at this point to give that of the Pali word 'buddha': the awakened one, or he who has awoken. There is therefore a link between the first requirement of supervision and the Buddhist concept of 'mindfulness' which is so prevalent nowadays.

Similarly, the group seems to be struggling to find the right approach in this session with John. A lot of different perspectives are offered, and a range of questions are being asked. Then one group member notices that John has used the word 'poaching' where he meant to say 'coaching', and she wonders whether there is any significance to that. Another, non-English, group member checks if that would mean chasing the client with the aim of obtaining trophies or tusks. John seems disinterested, doesn't seem to recognise this slip, nor see the word 'poaching' as particularly relevant. Soon after, another group member makes an apparently unrelated observation: 'I am not sure what the group is doing here. It seems we are just going down various rabbit holes and not getting anywhere,' and John nods ever so slightly. Then the same non-native speaker as before says, 'You mean like in "poaching" for rabbits?'

All of a sudden there is a link for John who thinks aloud about how he might be going down rabbit holes with his client, groping about for potentially useful interventions. This heralds a major shift for John and a major shift for the group at the same time. Suddenly everyone seems to recognise the image of poaching (coaching for one's own benefit and not for the client's) and similarly that of going down rabbit holes (looking nervously in many directions, in the hope of obtaining some 'instant insight'). Certainly for John something transformative happens, as he realises some of what he has been doing, plus the need to put the contract with his client on a different footing and to endeavour to tune more deeply into what the client really needs from him.

Modalities of reflection

We can see forms of reflection as tones or modalities of a piece of music called supervision. A fine structure in terms of harmony (bringing together of modalities of reflection) and melody (succession of modalities of reflection) gives a supervision session the richness that is required for new insights and actions. A thorough examination of the 'state of things' within coaching and consulting relationships means discussing a variety of facets and bringing together and confronting old and new reflections. It is important to break out of the repetition or slumber of a period of inflexible reflection and, so to speak, to wake up singing with a different pitch and tune.

Reflection has many aspects, simply because reflecting thoroughly means shifting between perspectives and rising above limited, inward-looking, defensive ways of seeing. In a dialogue, reflection means not only allowing the other person's perspective but actually taking it on board, without immediately dismissing or suppressing it, nor embracing it without question. To illustrate the richness of reflection and of the 'reflective path', this section discusses three models of reflection all of which place an emphasis on a 'tao' of reflection, a path with many different stages or levels.[4] We will spend a little

---

[4] The old Chinese word *tao* or *dao* has a variety of meanings, ranging from more prosaic terms related to development (the path, the way somewhere or the doctrine), to more philosophical usage (the 'just' path, the 'right' doctrine, perfection or enlightenment as the outcome of development). I use the word here because the authors cited in this chapter who describe paths of reflection often appear to have both areas of meaning in mind.

longer on the most recent one of these, because it allows for different modalities or tones of reflection at the same time. This model therefore gives us the option of moving to and fro between processes of reflection, or sticking to one particular position while at the same time being open to reflection in other ways, as we often see in supervision.

CASE EXAMPLE

The supervisee comes in as agreed, talks about the background to her consulting assignment and reads out a detailed account of a recent consulting session that was part of that assignment (see the classical supervision method in Chapter 6). When she stops reading and looks at the supervisor expectantly, she seems slightly deflated but alert at the same time. The supervisor asks: 'And what are your feelings towards this client?' The supervisee is silent for a while and then responds: 'Well . . . I dreamed about this assignment last night. My boss showed me a letter, from the sponsor, saying that the client wasn't able to continue with me and had requested a different consultant from our office.'

Further questions reveal that something similar had been said right at the start of the assignment. Doubts had been expressed about the 'quality' or 'suitability' of this consultant, the supervisee. She had kept this to herself for a long time while feeling pretty awful about the idea that she 'wasn't wanted' in this assignment.

As in the written text, the consultant's reflections in the supervision session seem to be very entrenched. Time and again, supervisor and supervisee come back to basically positive feelings towards the client, and deep anxiety about a possible rejection. It seems impossible to gain a fresh perspective on the case. For example, it seems impossible to think in a negative or critical way about the client. And it seems impossible to put a possible rejection by the client into perspective.

The first model of reflection, which comes from Carl Rogers (1958), crystallises a recognisable phenomenon in 'helping' conversations, namely that clients develop more self-confidence and openness as they go through such conversations, and gain more nerve to expose themselves to their own reflection as well as loosen up or become more spontaneous (see Table 3.1). The model starts with those 'clients' who don't show up because they don't think they have any problems or because helping conversations per se inspire too much anxiety in them. Then there are the clients who do show up but then ascribe their problems to others. It is sometimes only with enormous difficulty that these clients can be induced to look at themselves and their own responsibility. Usually, this succeeds only when they experience major problems outside the sessions or feel particularly safe within the sessions, but even then they remain entrenched in a sort of 'tourist' attitude. They look at problems, other people, themselves and helping conversations with a degree of focus and curiosity, but with an attitude of general detachment, as if none of it ultimately has much to do with them. Only by overcoming this attitude can we truly enter into helping conversations and reflect on the successes and setbacks in our practice.

Table 3.1 Rogers' model of reflective phases

Step	Reflective skill	Reflection focused on . . .	Relational perspective, or degree of 'connectivity'
1	None/rigid	Survival: no recognition of problems, feelings, meaning; no desire to change	Not connected: communication about 'distant things' only
2	Aloof, fragile	Survival: problems *are* recognised, but as being external; not as one's own responsibility	Concrete sense-making
3	Declarative (I am . . ., I feel . . .)	Change and improvement: recognition of problems, feelings and meaning there and then. Shame and stress around feelings here and now	Interactive, communicative
4	Reflection after the event; start of here and now reflection	Accepting and learning: reflection on more personal feelings. Feelings, questions, curiosity, some taking of responsibility	Start of a deeper connection
5	Reflection now, discovery	Experiencing feelings here and now: struggling with feelings, taking responsibility and accepting ambivalence	Connected to the other person (true dialogue)
6	Living, lively reflection	Release, spontaneity, presence. Direct experiencing of feelings and self. Embodied sense of feelings. Problems are fully experienced	Connected to self and the other person, here and now
7	Reflecting while experiencing (reflexivity)[5]	Confidence in self and in the process, however contradictory or vague and however much of a struggle. Freshness, flexibility, vulnerability	Universally connected (to self, others, anyone)

Rogers' model of the therapeutic process ends with clients who know the benefits of helping conversations very well. They don't need helping conversations, yet aren't afraid of them. These clients continue, with a sense of awe and courage, with a learning attitude and with integrity, ready to benefit from helping conversations be they with colleagues, supervisors or anyone else who can teach them something.

Rogers' approach moves from complete stasis, absolutism and entrenchment to an ultimate flexibility and ease based on a large measure of self-knowledge. Table 3.1 gives an overview of this model. Those who find themselves mainly on the first two steps are not yet 'ready' for helping conversations, while those on the third step are still reflecting in too concrete, defensive and detached a way for supervision.[6]

[5] There are many definitions of reflexivity in the social sciences. Here, I use the term to mean a way of reflecting that takes account of the activity of reflecting itself and our own presuppositions during reflection.

[6] I use my own words here to describe the steps that Rogers writes about, at the risk of attributing a different meaning to the seven steps or stages of the conversation process, because Rogers' terminology is strongly biased towards therapy. The many examples in Rogers (1958) are well worth consulting, as are those in the publications of Torbert (2004) and Carroll (2010) which are discussed later.

The second model, from Torbert (2004), a model of reflection-in-action and of making decisions in the moment, also contains seven stages of reflection, which also lead to greater looseness and flexibility. Here, however, each step includes the previous one as an option. The supervisee can therefore move back and forth in the hierarchy of modalities, but only up to the level that they have accomplished. In other words, each step takes us to a new reflective skill, while all previous modalities continue to be available. According to Torbert, many people get stuck for good halfway along the path towards deep, penetrating reflection. Table 3.2 shows the seven steps, again running from two reflective attitudes focused more on survival than on development to what (according to Torbert) is an extremely rare form of meta-reflection and the use of a multiplicity of perspectives.

However much insight they provide, Rogers' and Torbert's models assume that we as professionals go through all of the various stages and become a better person and a better consultant in the process. In a way, these models allow you to measure people against a yardstick. However, reality is more complex in my view. I find it more realistic to see obstacles and breakthroughs in reflection as parallel: in certain respects, the supervisee or supervisor may engage in very subtle and bold reflection, while in other respects the reflections fall far short of the task or assignment under discussion.

Carroll's model of reflective modalities or positions (2010) has the advantage that it explores a wide spectrum of steps, without saying that we have to follow them all or even that certain reflections are better than others – even though there are always 'under-reflections' and 'over-reflections' – i.e. aspects on which you are not allowing yourself any reflection at all and aspects to which your thoughts constantly return

Table 3.2 Torbert's model of reflective modalities

Step	Reflective skill	Reflection focused on . . .	Relational perspective, or degree of 'connectivity'
1	Opportunistic	Control of the organisation/outside world	Power and control over others
2	Diplomatic	Adjusting to and fitting in with the organisation/outside world	Self-control and connection through cooperation
3	Expert	Cognitive understanding of (aspects of) the organisation/outside world	Connection by doing things carefully and well (efficiency)
4	Achievement-oriented	Outcomes and results, influence and collaboration, use of personal feedback	Connection by doing the right things (effectiveness)
5	Individualistic	Critical consideration, taking account of self, conflict, emotions, dilemmas, uncertainty	Connected by making a personal contribution
6	Strategic	Reflection itself, via meta-reflection and reflexivity	Connected to self and the other person, by means of role choice and role negotiation
7	'Alchemistic'	Holding multiple perspectives; sense-making through metaphors	Connected on various levels, including morality and general humanity

Table 3.3   Carroll's model of reflective modalities

Tone	Reflective skill	Reflection focused on . . .	Relational perspective, or degree of 'connectivity'
1	Zero	Myself	Not connected
2	Empathic	The other person(s)	Empathically connected
3	Relational	Myself *and* the other person(s)	Interpersonal
4	Systemic	Myself, other person(s), *and* the environment	Contextual
5	Self-reflective	Meta-perspective on myself	Internally connected, incorporated
6	Transcendental	Meta-perspective on others and myself	Universally connected

without there being any development. Table 3.3 gives a brief overview of Carroll's model, and below is a summary of the six modalities (tones) of reflection that he differentiates, including the main differences between these various 'tones'.

Tone 1

Tone 1 is actually unreflective. This modality circles around the same idea: that I am right and other people wrong. This idea is usually concrete, factual, black-and-white and linear in its attributions. For example: 'This client is too demanding and doesn't understand what we're working on. As a result we haven't been able to hold a single interview yet.' A person in tone 1 uses supervision to get someone or something in his environment to change. For example: 'How can I pass over the client and find another sponsor in the organisation?' The supervisee doesn't implicate himself. The manner of presenting is often 'unconversational', more a monologue of statements based on the assumption that 'everyone understands' them to be absolutely true. This all sounds fairly primitive and simplistic, and indeed it is, but it would be naive to assume that our fully-fledged, experienced, reflective supervisees, or we ourselves as supervisors, never end up in this modality. We probably do so every day, over all sorts of trifling issues, but unfortunately over more important ones as well. Just under the surface of tone 1 there is often concern or shame about the fact that we are not 'up to' the problem.

Tone 2

Tone 2 is the reflective attitude that looks at a situation from two angles. In such circumstances there is an empathy for and (an attempt to gain) an understanding of the other person or persons. The principal idea is that what the other person has done *can* be understood, but not excused. The supervisee still adopts an untouchable position, from which he starts to reflect on the other person. For example: 'I do understand why my client makes such a fuss, cancels appointments, shows up late and doesn't listen properly when I say something – circumstances in his company are very difficult at the moment – but that doesn't alter the fact that he needs to motivate himself better.' This 'tone' is characterised by empathy, but often without compassion. There is more flexibility and even a degree of uncertainty or doubt, but the manner of presenting is still largely one-way traffic, or feels like a discussion rather than a conversation. Supervisees position themselves outside the problem and are incapable of imagining that they themselves might be part of it. Just under the surface there is still the fear of losing control or 'not knowing'.

Tone 3

Tone 3 is the reflective attitude that can look at a relationship as an interactive endeavour or a constant giving and taking in interaction, with causality moving away from a linear one-way declaration. There are always at least two good reasons why something has happened, and at least two contributions to an underlying problem for which both have responsibility. The supervisee contributes a situation in a more detached way and wonders what he himself can do to help the other person move forward. For example: 'I have the feeling that we always get bogged down in our sessions, that he treats me like one of the many people he manages and that I am intimidated by his authority.' The manner of presenting is more considered, more open and more exploratory than in tones 1 and 2. Where in tones 1 and 2 the problem is usually localised in the other person or persons, here we see problems as being produced in a relationship. The conversation truly takes on the nature of a reflective dialogue in which both the person himself and the other people are scrutinised.

Tone 4

Tone 4 is the reflective attitude that looks at a context in which patterns can be observed. Here, bilateral relationship patterns are related to each other, resulting in multi-causality and relationality – i.e. thinking about relationships in terms of psychological undercurrents and as reflections of other relationships (the parallel process). The supervisee brings in a situation from a meta-perspective, whereby question and answer, problem and solution, situation and cause are more loosely connected. Judgement on what is going on here is deferred, and remains deferred, even in the making of attributions. For example: 'In the session I noticed that I started to defend my advice and that my client only became quieter and more critical as a result. I wonder why is it that we both struggle so much with this situation? Is there perhaps something else going on, something I'm not aware of?' The manner of presenting is much more enquiring, more searching and less 'eager' in terms of defending one's own answers and finding new ones. Deeper frustrations and doubts are expressed more easily. The session becomes a quest for issues and patterns that play a role in the bigger picture. The participants interpret in terms of the organisational culture and background of the consultant. Vague intuitions of the supervisor meet with much more of a response.

Tone 5

Tone 5 can be described as honest, uncompromising self-reflection. This is the modality where we really manage to incorporate all the signals around us into our 'learning agenda', into an accurate and completely open assessment of our own role in relationships, systems and organisations. Now the last lines of defence have been overcome and we are able to look at ourselves honestly and focus on the only thing we can actually change: our own contribution to relationships and situations. The supervisee brings in an agenda that concerns himself, composed of experiences and reflections on those experiences. For example: 'I know now that I don't feel good when promoting or "selling" my consulting services: partly because I imagine that other people have to decide for themselves if they need me and partly because I'm rather shy and uncertain in new relationships. And perhaps also because I think I'm "too good" for that. How can I adopt an attitude in initial encounters that is honest and sincere, and that answers understandable questions that clients may have during the first few sessions?' The manner of presenting sometimes resembles an internal deliberation which illustrates that the supervisee is prepared to accept full responsibility for his own role in situations and networks.

Tone 6

Tone 6 contains the reflections that go even further, which we must therefore describe as 'transpersonal', existential, philosophical, religious or spiritual. It is the reflective attitude that is concerned with sense-making itself, and hence undiluted meta-reflection. We work in tone 6 when we look at the bigger picture in which our working and learning takes place and ask ourselves what we effectively contribute in a deeper sense, and how tenable and sound that contribution actually is. The supervisee brings more existential doubts concerning all the areas of his own life, or the seeking of meaning in his own career. For example: 'I really wonder what I do it all for. I know that I and my clients have good lives, and that we all improve as a result of our collaboration, but I often find myself thinking about all those people who don't have access to a coach, or about the continuing polarisation and dumbing-down that goes on all around us. At the start that used to distract me, but now it's increasingly becoming the central issue.' The manner of presenting is sincere and open and usually shows that a great deal of internal reflective work has been done before bringing the issue to supervision.

Most readers will have recognised themselves in all six modalities of reflection, and that is indeed my own experience in working with consultants and coaches. As Carroll (2010) puts it, we actually have all of these modalities in us, but it is often difficult to use them all freely when faced with a critical, unresolved issue. We often entrench ourselves in one of the six tones.[7]

It should be clear that, as we rise up the 'scale', the nature of our reflections becomes more and more commendable: we involve others in the reflections, we become more frank towards ourselves, and our reflections evolve along more ethical and spiritual lines. However, this is deceptive in my experience because the risk of 'as if' reflections (lazy, comfortable, proud, hypocritical or self-important reflections) also increases accordingly. We all know examples of people who achieve advanced levels of

[7] Another aid to help us break loose from reflections in a limited domain is the 'seven eye' model for supervision proposed by Hawkins and Shohet (2006), where the seven 'eyes' represent the domain of the client, the domain of coaching/consulting interventions, the domain of the client–supervisee relationship, the domain of the supervisee, the domain of the supervisee–supervisor relationship, the domain of the supervisor and the wider context.

development in philosophical or spiritual terms while their self-image and image of others around them fails to rise above tone 1. In addition, in tones 5 and 6 there is a high risk of navel-gazing or free-flowing fantasy, with the result that reflections are not founded on actual experience and, in a way, start to lead a life of their own quite separate from any experience or action. The risk of under-reflection is a defining feature of tone 1 and the risk of over-reflection lies in wait in the last three tones.

CASE EXAMPLE

An organisation consultant presents a recent session with his client that he has written out. He has a good feeling about it and believes it may herald an important break-through in the assignment because he managed to get the client really thinking for the first time. He reads out his account of the session to the supervisory group. When he stops reading, a long, awkward silence ensues. The other members of the group seem to be frowning and the supervisor says nothing. It seems a while before anyone says anything and the group finds something in the account that they can reflect on.

One of the group members says that the account seems so full, so complete, that she has nothing to add to it. Then come the first questions: 'Where is your client in this account?' 'It seems to be full of your own brilliant inspirations, are you sure your client is ready for them?' 'Are you dissatisfied with your client?' And so on. The supervisee feels ashamed, guilty, inadequate. How could he ever have thought that this was a successful consulting session? Now he himself starts to look troubled and frowns, and the group reacts to that in turn. Someone suggests allowing more silences in future consulting conversations, and asking more questions about what is really preoccu-pying the client. Noticing the supervisee's subdued demeanour, the other group members start to feel guilty in turn. The supervisee leaves the meeting with a feeling of dejection, of irritation with himself and the others.

It is only the next day that he develops some perspective on what happened during the supervision. Perhaps the feeling of shame and the criticism he read between the lines is a parallel process and his client felt the same in the consulting session with him? There doesn't seem to be any end as yet to the spiral of guilt and penance, of criticism and shame.

A few days later he tells a colleague what happened during the supervision. His colleague suggests that his account of the session may have come across as so successful and so complete that the others in the group were jealous. That hadn't occurred to him, and he then wonders if jealousy is also at play in his relationship with his client. Only then does he feel somewhat reassured.

In the last case example we see an organisation consultant jumping from tone 1 to tones 2 and 3 and then really struggling in tone 5. Only much later, in tone 4, do things start to fall into place and is he able to rise above the difficult nature of this supervision session while retaining the benefit of the hard lessons he has learned thus far. Sometimes a supervision session can have effects on our reflections that persist for weeks afterwards, only later generating a degree of insight and clarity.

Caroll's model gives a number of possible obstructions versus breakthroughs that can indeed take place in supervision – and in other forms of personal learning.

- The ability to move from one tone to the next. For example, supervisees who move from 1 to 2 are suddenly able to draw a different perspective into reflection. Or, in moving from 4 to 5, they are able to look at themselves in a new way, more as an instrument that can have a particular 'function' or be 'of service'.
- The ability to find more 'overtones' within a given 'tone'. For example, supervisees manage to identify different motives in another person in tone 2, or different patterns in their own organisation in tone 4 – factors they were previously unaware of.
- The ability to 'disengage' from even very valuable reflections. It helps to move backwards and forwards in the model and to let go of any reflections that arise, but this doesn't guarantee that the supervisee will ultimately heed the changes indicated by the supervision and implement them in practice.

Obstacles to these abilities are often expressed as 'defences': rejecting different ways of seeing because they come too close to certain sensitivities. These sensitivities are based on a degree of shame, embarrassment or vulnerability. Defences come in many forms (for a summary, see Chapter 8 of de Haan and Burger 2005).

Often, however, precisely the opposite is the case: supervision can dredge up old perspectives that had disappeared below the surface and shed new light on them. Or a certain long-held perspective, when compared with a different 'tone', fades away into the background – for example, when we forget and ignore ourselves completely as consultants and become engrossed in helping our clients as effectively as possible. When we suddenly add a reflection on tone 1 in a situation like this, it can bring a significant breakthough. We suddenly become aware of our own needs and how they may be sacrificed. Or we remember the simple fact that we have needs. This happens when we realise that we should actually just say 'no' to a new follow-up assignment – for example, where the new client is competing with another department in the same organisation we are already consulting to. While for Rogers and Torbert the most mature or sensible way of reflecting is represented by the 'highest' level, for Carroll it is the art of moving flexibly through and between all six different levels.

Reflection always has elements of freedom in restraint, of breaking a cage around our current thinking and hence erecting a new cage. Reflections liberate just as much as they entrap. That is the main difference between reflection and navel-gazing. Navel-gazing doesn't touch the boundaries of our encaged thinking and feeling, while reflection can break open those boundaries, at least temporarily. In my view, the greatest enemy of reflection is thinking you're already there. How often does it happen in a supervision session that, just when the supervisor has the impression that an important reflection or a new way of doubting is patently obvious, the supervisee avoids it by saying something like: 'Thanks, supervisor, that's all very useful. And I also wanted to talk about . . .'

Supervisors often struggle just as much with reflection as do their supervisees, or are even more surprised than them at a breakthrough in reflection. So it is not correct to assume that the supervisor is a step ahead or that he moves throughout the model completely freely. The only (major) advantage that supervisors have is that supervision is not about their practice, so the reflections hit much less close to home and it remains easier for them to take a critical stance. Nevertheless, they still have their own blind spots, can be dogmatic, and sometimes have inhibitions about entering certain tones in the reflect on model – for example, having the courage to think with a systemic focus, to reflect on sexual aspects of relationships, to feel helpless or to permit existential doubts during supervision. The supervisor–supervisee dyad often moves as a unit within the model and as a result frequently gets stuck in a given tone without anyone realising it.

CASE EXAMPLE

Helen arrives at her first supervision session with a transcript made from an audio recording of a recent coaching session. She reads it out and the supervisor listens, occasionally making notes. The sense the supervisor makes of the session is of a competent and professional exploration. Helen appears to allow her client to express himself naturally and she is not imposing any assumptions or views from her side. Probing a little deeper the supervisor observes that the coaching session appears somewhat shallow, something she attributes to the fact that the coach unquestioningly accepts the views, agenda and objectives of the client. The supervisor thinks she would herself perhaps have enquired into the main assumption of the client, that 'it is time now for him to move on, to a new career'. Is that really so? How can he be so sure?

The supervisor starts off the supervision by offering her first impression, feeding back the evidence of careful contracting and seamless exploration, paying a compliment for the sound summaries, the neutral stance and the open questions from within the frame of the client. Then, all of a sudden, rereading the transcript, she notices a small exception to this. When the client says, 'Perhaps we can look at what happens in my head when I hold back' the coach responds with, 'Right, let us do so. What are you feelings when you are in this state of holding back?' The supervisor remarks that head and feelings are not exactly the same thing. At this point it is as if a penny drops for Helen. She appears to greet this minor qualification (in the view of the supervisor) as an important insight, pulls out her notebook and starts making copious notes. And she thanks her supervisor who had not anticipated the comment would elicit such a response.

Later they talk about embracing all the assumptions of the client – both the (explicit, above the surface) intent to change career and the (implicit, below the surface) procrastination which indicates that the client is also ambivalent about it.

Carroll (2009) argues that it is a good idea, when drawing up a contract with new supervisees, to ask questions about how they reflect. Questions such as:

- How do you learn? How would you describe your learning style?
- How can I best facilitate your learning?

- What might I do that could block your learning? And what defences will we see as a result?
- How might differences between us affect your learning style?

The struggle to move from experience to compassion

It may sound presumptuous, but I do not believe there is any other way to achieve greater professionalism and compassion than by going through the 'scales of reflection'. As we know, animals are strangers to reflection. And at the other end of the spectrum stands Socrates, the man who, as tradition has it, had nothing but reflection. The Oracle at Delphi had declared Socrates the wisest man on earth. When he came to learn of this and investigated, it turned out that he owed his 'wisdom' solely to the fact that he considered and reflected on his own ignorance and folly, not to the fact that he knew anything that others didn't, because that wasn't the case. Socrates took a stand in favour of living reflection in all of his conversations. A famous quote in this context is 'The unexamined life is a life not worth living', as Plato has Socrates say in the *Apology* (38a).

But what is 'living reflection'? Is such a thing as living reflection actually possible? Are we really capable of studying our own lives? Are we capable of studying our own presuppositions and our reflections ourselves, including the distortions of those reflections? A reflective life means entering into and gathering experiences, and allowing those experiences to be scrutinised and stripped of all too easy presuppositions and preconceptions. It also involves the participation of others, such as the supervisor, who may pick up distortions and preconceptions more readily.

By breaking through barriers and moving through the various modalities outlined in the last section, we clear away defences. As a result, we move via new sense-making to novel ways of seeing and hence to new possibilities in terms of action. For example, what initially had the sense of a flop, loss or failure, or even a 'tragedy', can be viewed in a different light with the aid of reflection – for example, as a clearing of the decks to make way for new opportunities. The movement triggered by reflection, provided it is maintained consistently and with warmth and attention, leads automatically to more reflection and more movement, but also to forgiveness, clemency and compassion, for ourselves as much as for others.

Let us look in more detail at what happens on this reflective path. To this end, I will discuss an arbitrary example that is recognisable to many consultants.

CASE EXAMPLE: PROFESSIONAL DEVELOPMENT THROUGH LIVING REFLECTIONS

Step 1: unconsciously incompetent

Daniel is an organisation consultant. He rushes from assignment to assignment, from consulting session to interview, from presentation to focus group. He works well and with a great deal of enthusiasm, but is completely unaware of his unfortunate tendency to 'talk over' his clients at crucial moments. He is a good listener, quick-witted, with ample experience of similar assignments. But often when he thinks he is beginning to understand something or is presenting something important, he unwittingly gets carried away by his own enthusiasm. He doesn't listen so well, answers questions immediately without really considering the question or its background, and passionately adds new material when frowns or queries appear on the faces of his clients or colleagues. Many of those around him are aware of this tendency, and it is a problem for some of them. It makes it harder for them to work with Daniel or to take on his suggestions, even though his ideas are often good and helpful. In this respect Daniel himself is entirely in Carroll's tone (modality) 1: absence of reflection.

Step 2: consciously incompetent

There comes a day in Daniel's consulting practice when a client or colleague makes an unmistakable comment about his unfortunate tendency. Daniel starts to realise that he sometimes doesn't listen as well as he might, that he talks over his clients and repeats himself under pressure. In addition, he realises that there are circumstances in which he forgets to 'be' a consultant because he is too busy 'acting' the consultant.

He asks a number of colleagues and his supervisor how they see this. They agree that, yes, he does sometimes have that unfortunate tendency. He plans to stop doing it and from now on only to listen closely to clients and keep asking questions if they have queries or comments. That turns out to be not as easy as he thought. Daniel notices that he still often gets carried away by his enthusiasm. In addition, colleagues and friends seem to be coming to him more often with comments about what a poor listener he is or how he talks over people.

This is a painful phase for Daniel. It is precisely now that he develops the most defences. He starts to work harder to understand his clients 'Really Well'. Or he sticks his head in the sand and lets his colleagues facilitate the more challenging groups. He often hankers back to the comfort of just being a successful consultant. If there is reflection, it is fairly aggrieved and in tone 2, driven by exasperation about his smart-alec colleagues or himself and his lack of ability.

Step 3: reflection after the fact

At a certain point Daniel starts actually to reflect more deeply. He begins to think about his sessions, tries to follow his own patterns, makes notes in his notebook. He solicits more feedback from his colleagues and puts his name down for an open course in 'non-directive counselling' with the main theme of 'empathic listening', so getting his reflective abilities underway. At the same time he explores how prevalent his tendency is, what circumstances contribute to it, what alternatives he has and how he can assume a deeper, warmer, more authentic listening attitude.

He may also discuss this with his supervisor. The supervisor will help him to supplement his reflections in tone 5 (self-reflections) with more relational, systemic considerations. The supervisor may also explore whether, in a distant past, Daniel sometimes had to fight to make himself heard or was kept down by the strong opinions of his father and older brothers.

Step 4: 'l'esprit de l'escalier'

Daniel's curiosity and involvement in his own issue is now alive and active. He is developing not only a range of perspectives on his behaviour but also a number of alternative forms of action. In his consulting practice, he is still consciously incompetent for the most part, apart from some minor changes and adjustments and perhaps a few more jitters in his sessions with clients. But with the passing of time, with constant reflection and readiness, reflection after the event can now start slowly to evolve into reflection-in-action. A common phenomenon here is l'esprit de l'escalier, a term borrowed from the French philosopher Diderot which expresses the idea that, in certain situations, you realise what you should have done only after the event (see Chapter 5). Often just after a session with a client, Daniel realises that he's 'done it' again – that his inspiration has run away with him again or that he has turned away from the client at a crucial time in the session. He also knows exactly what he could, or should, have done in that session. For example, slowly repeat the question put to him there and then, at that precise moment, or pose a counter-question along the lines of 'Where does your doubt come from?' or 'Is there something missing for you in this account?'

During supervision, Daniel is fast developing a form of competence. He knows exactly which client session he wants to bring in. And he already knows what was actually going on in that session and what he could have done differently. The supervisor notices that Daniel is thus doing the supervisory work by himself and that a few brief summaries by the supervisor are sufficient to prompt fruitful reflection on a client relationship.

Step 5: reflection-in-action

Daniel is now, sometimes, consciously competent. He is able to reflect on the way he is listening even during difficult client sessions or presentations. This phenomenon is reflected initially in Daniel himself being quieter. Later, it is reinforced as he starts to involve his clients. He has done a 180° turn and has replaced the constant, implicit question 'Do you understand what I mean?' by 'Am I really understanding your meaning?' At the start it still sounds forced and slightly defensive, but as time goes on Daniel is able in an entirely natural way to pose counter-questions, raise hypotheses and offer summaries of the critical issues facing his partners in complex consulting processes.

Step 6: unconsciously competent

A few years later, Daniel has stopped anxiously observing himself in client sessions where his listening behaviour is put to the test. He acts naturally in client situations and is not afraid to take on a central role in meetings, interviews, presentations or conversations where bad news has to be broken. His clients and colleagues see him as a good listener, even in difficult circumstances, and are particularly impressed by his skill in maintaining a listening attitude under a storm of criticism or when calmly and attentively hearing out his biggest opponents; this has become second nature in a way. In particular, the picture of Daniel calmly taking out his notebook from his bag when strong criticism of the consulting process or the consultant is unexpectedly expressed during a summing-up or an evaluation round, stays with many colleagues.

Daniel may be changing, but the leopard hasn't changed his spots. He is the first to know it – for example, in the way he still gets carried away in a lecture, but also (if he is honest) in many a consulting or coaching session, on the tide of his own words, his passion, and his hypothesis that he still hopes, deep down, is the only right one, the universal truth that will have his clients singing his praises for years to come. So he acknowledges that there are still many times when he gets wrapped up in his own ideas and suggestions. But he is now able to conceal it better and has at least learned at such times to remain silent, to smile and nod affably, even if he is inwardly completely distracted.

Step 7: meta-reflection

True meta-reflection that actually takes place on a different level, and that marks a transition from tone 5 to tone 6, occurs only during the unconsciously competent phase, where Daniel has time to look at himself and notices when he becomes wrapped up in his own convictions. He has spent years exploring the theme of 'listening' for himself and has struggled, with the help of reflections, supervision and courses, to listen better and better precisely at those times when listening is under pressure and called for. And very gradually, overcoming fears and embarrassment, he has regained the nerve to focus on the listening of others around him. He has started to look again at the questions and criticisms raised by his clients, at his own counter-questions and summaries, and is slowly detaching himself from his own struggle to maintain his listening behaviour in situations of debate and misunderstanding. And he has reclaimed the nerve to ask how 'purely' his colleagues and clients are actually listening – the topic on which they have set him so much homework. Without being defensive himself, without investing too much in it, he starts to adopt a fresh perspective on the questions put to him concerning his consulting. And he becomes more and more aware, or perhaps differently aware, of the lack of understanding, defensive patterns, resistance and laziness that are sometimes associated with those questions. Because he is now less determined to defend his own consulting, he is able – after careful listening – to bring up that lazy and die-hard background to many questions. And as he does so, this time without seeking to defend or manifest his own advice, reputation or consulting role, he naturally develops compassion with the way his clients think. He realises that these are patterns that are also inherent in himself and that he has overcome only with difficulty and only in part. So he is aware of the extent to which client, sponsor, colleague and he himself share certain responses, how they all have good intentions but are all too quickly led astray, and how no one is immune to all-too-human failings, feelings of omnipotence and shame.

Daniel is now capable of being profoundly moved by what he shares, in the heat of a debate, presentation or consulting session, with his client, opponent, partner or 'target' of consulting. Moved by the way in which, from this perspective, in our inability to listen properly, let go of our own sacred cows and really reflect, we are all in fact cast in exactly the same mould. This is when Daniel develops compassion: compassion through reflection. Both compassion for himself as a consultant and for his colleagues and clients, as if the wide disparities in role between these parties disappear like snow in summer, giving way to deep similarities in general human endeavour, feeling, thought and action.

I hope this chapter has shown that reflection can really make a big difference to a supervisee. A series of important breakthroughs over many years of reflective work, combined with new experiences, can lead to a personality change. So we shouldn't treat reflections too lightly or take them for granted, any more than our everyday inspirations and discoveries. I believe that Torbert (2004) is right in saying that we run a real risk of persisting throughout our lives with the same unproductive reflections on a given topic. Indeed, a much more useful, positive, effective way of thinking can sometimes be just around the corner but remain inaccessible due to entrenched reflections and the defences around reflections. On the other hand, we shouldn't be too much in awe of 'paradigm-shifting', 'deadlock-breaking', 'deep, transformative insight-generating' reflections. Fundamentally new reflections occur almost by definition when 'reflection-in-relation' takes place, as during supervision. The other person in the room, the supervisor, will see certain things differently and come up with different perspectives and interpretations as a result. If you open yourself up to these as a supervisee, then new insight is in fact entirely possible in every supervision session.

Summary

The role of **supervisee** is generally more difficult than that of supervisor for professional consultants and coaches. What do you actually need to do to inhabit this role fully?

1   Literally 'wake up' and freshen up to a sharp and clear mindset.
2   Relate accounts about yourself, full of facts and feelings.
3   Play with those accounts: think up new perspectives and endings.
4   Look critically at facts and feelings in those accounts.
5   Listen to interruptions, interpretations and alternative accounts.

6   Admit and recognise that you have doubts, do not know some things and get stuck.

7   Choose new intentions and actions, with conviction.

The essence of good supervision for the supervisee is **reflection-in-relation**:

- Reflecting on reflection itself, based on reflection models and meta-perspectives.
- Relating the relationship itself, namely to client relationships and to other relationships of your clients and yourself.

Supervision sessions focus on finding the 'right' reflections: reflections that benefit the supervisee's clients – and their organisations. Sometimes this means developing new perspectives, or new insight. Sometimes it means letting go of old, entrenched reflections, or moving to a different **modality** of reflection.

Caroll (2010) differentiates the following **modalities (tones) of reflection**:

1   No reflections: focused on self and stuck to the old.

2   Empathic reflections: focused on the other person.

3   Relational reflections: focused on relationships.

4   Systemic reflections: focused on context and organisation.

5   Self-reflections: focused on the self but going beyond the personal framework.

6   Transcendent reflections: again going beyond the personal framework, now with regard to all of the above.

Supervisees are encouraged to move freely between these different modalities and, with the supervisor's help, to engage in **meta-reflection** on (the possibility of) lazy, entrenched and unsound reflections.

Supervisor and supervisee encounter **defences**, with which the supervisee:

- censures certain accounts or keeps them out of supervision completely;
- doesn't allow certain reflections;
- doesn't allow the consequences of certain reflections (new intention or action).

By means of **reflection-in-relation**, you can not only come up with all sorts of **useful ideas** for your clients but also develop more **warmth and compassion** which can really change you as a supervisee and a person.

How does reflection develop over time?

1 From unconsciously incompetent (not reflecting), to
2 painfully and consciously incompetent, realising one's own short-comings, to
3 reflection after the fact or reflection before action, e.g. during supervision, to
4 *l'esprit de l'escalier*, i.e. reflection just after the action, to
5 reflection in action, i.e. consciously competent, considering other actions during action, to
6 unconsciously competent, including lifting some reflection from action, to
7 meta-reflection, i.e. experiencing true compassion for oneself and others.

4 The organisation supervisor: shadow consulting in full colour

with David Birch

SUPERVISION AS...
A shadow consultant

The practice of supervision has been with us for over a century, but it is only in the last few decades that supervision has begun to make a contribution to organisations. Organisation development (OD) consultants are increasingly benefiting from supervision in their organisation consulting practice. Consulting professionals and their clients are increasingly seeing supervision as a true mark of quality and reliability for consulting services. With the continuing professionalism of the OD field, supervision is making an important contribution to professional qualifications. And as more and more organisation developers choose to set up their own practices or niche consultancies, the need for organised reflection increases. Within the well-established world of supervision for (one-to-one) counselling, therapy and coaching, the initial outlines of a new discipline are starting to form: *organisation supervision*.

In this chapter we look at various forms of organisation supervision and the contributions they make to organisations, while also reviewing the pros and cons of different supervision contracts. We end with a number of dilemmas that will be familiar to the practising organisation supervisor. We hope to show how organisation supervision is different from coaching supervision, and in some ways holds richer scope for reflection because of the additional layers of complexity.

We see organisation consulting or consulting-for-organisation-development as a broader field than coaching, comprising larger-scale organisational interventions such as process consultation, team and organisation development, strategic conferences and whole-system approaches. Consulting interventions that involve more people, departments and systems make organisation consultants work closer with the objectives and strategy of the client organisation and with their own 'client systems' within that organisation. Supervision therefore acquires a broader and deeper basis, even if, as is usually the case, it takes place 'off-line' – i.e. outside the organisation. To put it briefly, organisation supervision is much more complex, multi-layered and diverse than coach supervision, as we will attempt to show in the models and examples given in this chapter. It is for this reason that organisation supervision usually branches out into more areas of the professional's role, encompassing the way in which the consultant or supervisee interacts with other consultants within the context of assignments or with the consultant's 'home base' – i.e. the consultancy to which he is affiliated. Organisation supervision also touches on organisational dynamics within consulting teams and consultancies, as a result of which parallel processes extend to parallels between entire organisations or systems: the 'customer system' may somehow be reflected in the 'consulting system'. In other words, organisation supervision is sometimes focused not on the consultants' clients at all, but rather on the consultants' relationships with their direct peers and managers in their own companies, yet always with a view to improving their own effectiveness as a consultant in client organisations.

Three forms of organisation supervision

Organisation developers do their work within organisations while holding on to their outsider's perspective. They apply their knowledge, experience and intuition while forming a picture of what is going on in the organisation. In so doing, they often quickly develop an 'insider's perspective', or different 'insider's perspectives'. Such a stance of being an 'outsider within' is not straightforward at all, and carries with it all sorts of temptations, risks and limitations (de Haan 2006). The most crucial of these is a 'Scylla and Charybdis' between, on the one hand, the risk of staying overly distant and analytical, culminating in observations, ideas and solutions that are more relevant for the consultant – or for his previous clients – than for the case in point; and on the other hand the risk of over-identifying and becoming engrossed in the agenda and issues within the assignment. In other words, organisation developers are constantly exposed to the dilemma of 'aloofness versus collusion'. Supervision can offer support in this respect: reflection helps to maintain the right balance between opposing risks and temptations.

The supervisor stays – as much as possible – outside of the client relationship, and hence is much freer to comment on what might be going on for the client (or client organisation) and between the consultant and the client (or client organisation). Supervision can have an immense formative effect on consultants and contribute to the monitoring of standards and strengthening of consulting skills (i.e. as a developer, gate-keeper or nurse – see Chapter 1). Organisation consultants often experience tensions, not only between their feelings and attitudes within and outside the organisations they work with, but also between their work and their private lives, and between the competing obligations to varying parties and clients within a portfolio of activities and assignments. Supervision helps to reduce these stresses by allowing the consultant to reflect on his own practice more freely and with greater detachment, including detachment from his own reactions and sensitivities. Moreover, the supervisor is in an ideal position to help to manage a consultant's practice, based on the appreciation of the struggles and challenges within that practice that comes automatically from joint reflection. The supervisor's understanding of what is going on within that practice and where the tensions come from is often better than that of the consultant's line manager, or even the consultant himself.

The organisation supervisor and organisation consultant can work together in three different contracts or relationships: organisation consulting supervision, shadow consulting and peer supervision.

Organisation consulting supervision

This form of supervision is fully focused on the individual consultant and his practice. The supervisor is not part of the consultant's organisation, or of the organisations to which the consultant provides services, so he is in a unique position to observe the dynamics between these organisations, including the patterns of transference and counter-transference that are inherent to consulting assignments and supervisory relationships (Searles 1955; Ledford 1985). Because he has no direct experience of the consulting environment, the supervisor can have confidence that his own observations and impressions can only be shaped by the supervisee in this session (and previous sessions), and are therefore free from his own resonance with the consulting environment. This gives the supervisor's reflections during the sessions added value: what he is observing and feeling as the supervision progresses must be relevant to the client organisation and the consultant's approach, possibly in conjunction with patterns within his own consulting organisation. The supervisee can therefore have confidence that he is meeting a reasonably 'clean' sounding board, relatively free from competition, envy, own experiences, recollections, desires and aspirations. The supervisor then helps the supervisee freely to investigate his own associations, impressions, emotions, assumptions, prejudices and decisions.

CASE EXAMPLE

Roger is a consultant working for a niche consultancy who has been involved for a number of years in the projects managed by five partners. He is one of the 15 senior consultants and is generally seen as someone with partner potential, although no explicit course towards that level of responsibility has been mapped out for him. The consultancy pays for him to meet with a clinical psychologist for around four supervision sessions a year.

Although they talk about Roger's clients and consultancy portfolio during supervision, it is more usually about the dynamics within the firm. For example, Roger finds it difficult that differences of opinion between the partners are sometimes apparent but are suppressed in public, so that they are mainly played out explicitly as conflict between the senior consultants. The partners do their best to maintain the pretence that they are always in agreement. They meet every month and although everyone knows when and where those meetings take place, no one knows exactly what goes on there or how developments and career paths within the firm are discussed. Symbolically, the nature of these meetings is nicely summed up by the door to the library, which normally stands open but is firmly shut during partner meetings.

Roger regularly feels criticised by one of the partners. When this happens, another partner normally extends a hand in support and encouragement, but without speaking to the first partner. Roger also notices that he is often mentioned in the same breath as another senior consultant, as if he is seen as competing with him for a single partnership position. These put-downs and rivalries within the firm are much harder for Roger than his client work, however intense he sometimes finds that to be.

As an outsider and an independent party, the supervisor 'holds up the mirror' in a way that helps Roger to appreciate his own part in the dynamics more clearly. For example, Roger learns how some of his reactions are understandable in terms of his own family dynamics, and the fact that he feels relatively vulnerable within the firm while he feels much more impactful and confident when working with his clients. As a result of the supervision sessions, he comes to understand the situation and manages to steer a steady course without letting any of the tensions escalate too far. And after a number of years he is indeed invited to become a partner. It is only then that he suddenly becomes aware of how far the tensions and uncertainties between the partners go. In view of the more open rivalries at partner level, he considers it useful to continue his individual supervision relationship for a few more years.

Shadow consulting

Shadow consulting (Schroder 1974) is a form of supervision for a consultant or a team of consultants that focuses on supporting a consultancy project actively from an 'off-line' supervisory perspective. As in organisation consulting supervision, the client organisation does not encounter the supervisor, except perhaps as a name on a contract or invoice. The consulting organisation does tend to notice shadow consulting, because it is an active part of (some) consulting assignments. The supervisor works away from the glare of the consultancy assignment, literally in the 'shadow' of the consulting team, looking for new shades, colours and patterns within the team that can be traced to the consulting work. This detachment from the client system enables the supervisor to pick up in particular some (counter-)transference that slips the consultants' notice. The situation often gives rise to parallel processes (Searles 1955) in which teams of consultants unwittingly repeat patterns that originate in the client organisation, especially patterns that neither they nor their clients have really examined or reflected on. It is due to the natural amplification during supervision that patterns like these, which often represent crucial obstacles to the assignment and the intended organisational change, first come to light.

A shadow consultant is usually attached to a team of consultants for the duration of a consulting project or for its initial stages in which it is most vital to understand and get to grips with the organisational dynamics. Shadow consultants often come from the consultancy itself. Shadow consulting can also take place in mixed groups of consultants or on an ad hoc basis.

CASE EXAMPLE

An organisation consultant was asked to lead the supervision of a team of external change consultants managing a change process at a major financial services firm. As the first group supervision session progressed, the supervisor noticed that whenever the team leader was speaking, her mind wandered. Even when she forced herself to listen, she was only able to follow what he was saying for a few minutes before her attention was diverted again. When others in the team spoke, she found it much easier to concentrate but was concerned about the quality of her supervision because she hadn't followed a lot of what the team leader had said.

When the same thing happened during the second supervision meeting, the organisation supervisor decided to share her experience with the group in a way that avoided criticising the team leader. She asked whether others felt the same way and whether this might be a reflection of their work with the organisation in some way. To her astonishment several team members admitted that they too found it hard to follow their team leader's argument. The team leader himself was initially embarrassed, but with the help of the group came to realise that their key client, the chief executive, was a lone operator and generally seen as detached. It also emerged that various members of the managing board had told the change consultants that they only half understood what the chief executive wanted and what the actual objectives of the change process were. The supervisor pointed out that the impression the consulting team had of their leader was a textbook example of a parallel process in an organisation consulting assignment; in other words, what was going on here could be seen as a replica of what was happening in the client organisation.

The supervisor then helped the team think through what their project leader could do differently and how this insight might also be relevant to the chief executive. This resulted in a profound shift in the consulting team's effectiveness, producing incisive and useful feedback for the chief executive and good ideas for better communication surrounding the change process within the organisation. However, the most important shift took place within the team of consultants itself, because they also started to share other observations that could be construed as critical or negative. They developed a team spirit of mutual enquiry and reflection based on much more open feedback.

When the team leader raised his observations with the chief executive, the latter was similarly embarrassed and even defensive at first. Later, however, he was surprised and shocked when he sought feedback from his 'right-hand man' and he confirmed all of their observations down to the smallest detail.

Peer supervision

Peer supervision is a way of organising supervision within a consulting project. Consultants from the team can be allocated the role of supervisor/shadow consultant, or the supervisory role can rotate within the team. The advantage of peer supervision is that the peer supervisor has his own direct experience of the client organisation(s), from which he has taken away certain hunches and impressions that he can use freely during the supervision. The disadvantage is that the supervisor's ability to pick up unconscious patterns and parallel processes from the consulting team is highly compromised. It is therefore advisable for a peer supervisor working within a consulting team to call in an individual external supervisor for himself. The peer supervisor must be able to straddle all sorts of boundaries between consulting, supervision and participation in his own consulting team, and individual supervision can help him to maintain the various roles.

For us, the most effective method of peer supervision involves the peer supervisor remaining somewhat detached from his colleagues' consulting work, making time and space for formal supervision meetings held away from the client organisation and the work entailed in the assignment. The team of consultants will work best if there is clear contracting between them about the purpose of supervision and the roles adopted during supervision meetings.

CASE EXAMPLE

A team of 15 consultants working on a culture change project at a government department were grouped into five peer supervision groups, or 'trios'. Each trio met once a fortnight, usually via a teleconference, with the three colleagues taking it in turns to play the role of the supervisor.

In one trio, a consultant was concerned about the management style of one of the senior client staff, which he felt was unnecessarily aggressive and bullying. With the help of the peer supervisor and the third member of the trio, this consultant explored his feelings and reactions concerning the senior manager, including his unacknowledged prejudice associated with the manager's educational and social background. This helped the consultant to empathise with the manager and re-evaluate his own critical stance. Rather than confront the manager as he had been intending to, he decided that he would try to build a closer relationship with him and, if necessary, influence from a position of more openness, equality and respect.

Having introduced the three models of organisation supervision, here is a case example within one of them, shadow supervision. This example should illustrate the subtleties of consulting supervision assignments, including the fact that the consulting organisation and the client organisation can influence each other in hidden and unexpected ways, which can be brought out with the help of the supervisor as a detached but reflective outsider.

CASE EXAMPLE: SHADOW SUPERVISION

Gerard was an external consultant in an assignment involving around 10 different consultants at a top research institute. The aim of the assignment was to engage the academic staff and to motivate them to participate actively in the institute's research strategy and planning. During his involvement as a consultant and coach Gerard suddenly became aware that he was avoiding contact with another member of the consulting team called Sophie. This surprised and troubled him as they usually worked extremely well together. He felt that Sophie was disinterested in him and his ideas and seemed intent on expanding her own influence in the client organisation. This impression was reinforced by the close relationship that Sophie had established with a director of the research institute who had an outstanding international reputation as a leader of research programmes.

Gerard knew that he ought to raise his concerns with Sophie but felt uneasy and anxious at the prospect of doing so. He had convinced himself that Sophie would ridicule or humiliate him in the consulting team if he brought the subject up. Not only was he feeling shut out, he felt that he was failing in Sophie's eyes, as if she had heard something from her contacts in the institute about his weak points as a consultant.

Eventually it was Sophie who brought up the topic with Gerard, because she was as concerned as he was that their interactions had grown so distant. Gerard remained reluctant to engage with her but agreed that it would be a useful topic to take to the next meeting with the team supervisor, the project's shadow consultant.

The shadow consultant called a special session with Gerard and Sophie. He helped them to make connections with the consulting assignment itself and the relationships within the client organisation. The supervisor soon discovered that both Gerard and Sophie had come to identify strongly with their respective clients in the research institute. Sophie did indeed have a rapport with the senior professor who was highly influential in shaping the university's research agenda and the interpretation of their consulting assignment. Gerard meanwhile had established an equally strong bond with a less prominent research director, a professor who was expected to take on the administrative tasks and to be responsible for the success of part of the research agenda. Gerard had heard from his client about how the other professor showed little interest in his ideas and contributions and about how his client felt 'used' to do the dirty work within the institute. The supervisor suggested that what was going on between Gerard and Sophie gave a good indication of how the relationship between the two professors felt for the professors themselves. During the shadow consulting the three consultants explored how, in a parallel process, the relationship between two senior professors was reflected and recreated between these two consultants within the team.

Further exploration generated useful ideas about how Sophie and Gerard might work more effectively with the research institute. At the supervisor's instigation, they tried out a role-play in which they each took the role of their respective client. In what proved to be an enjoyable process, they used their intuition to depict how their clients and perhaps others in the organisation were feeling about each other and the new research agenda. To Gerard's surprise, Sophie was adamant in the role-play that 'her' professor would have been horrified to know that his colleague was so angry with him, which opened up a discussion about how the two professors could become more aware of their unconscious motives and patterns of behaviour.

Gerard and Sophie decided to work closely together in the run-up to the next workshop where a group of professors, including each of their clients, were encouraged to exchange strategic ideas and to build on existing suggestions for a new research agenda. Looking back at that workshop, the two professors were surprised at the different tone that prevailed in the session and the better understanding they had developed. The organisation decided to continue to use the same workshop model for the remainder of the strategy development process.

Gerard felt relieved that his strong relationship with Sophie had been restored. He was also satisfied with the fact that this exploration of extremely personal irritations, which he had initially thought had nothing to do with the consulting assignment, had led to such positive results within the relationship between the two professors and for the strategy development process. He realised that it would benefit him to capitalise on his irritations in one way or another in future assignments as well.

This example illustrates how a shadow consultant/supervisor can play an important role in helping consultants 'step back' temporarily from the drama of complicated assignments and explore their own assumptions, prejudices, irritations and unconscious signals. Such a move enables them to monitor their own ability to think clearly and reach a considered opinion on their client and their own teamwork. The shadow consultant/supervisor listens carefully to the organisation consultants' narratives, without actually believing them to be literally true or the 'whole truth'. With the aid of these narratives, he tracks down other narratives hidden just under the surface. He also helps the consultants to reframe these narratives by showing them how their participation in the client organisation has distorted and changed their capacity to think and act. These distortions themselves are always useful to learn from, and are not simply to be discarded.

Relational processes

Supervision for organisation consultants is a new field that is still expanding, on account of a growing recognition that professional consultants need space to attend to the relational processes that influence their competences and responses. The supervisor is in an excellent position to detect and explore such processes, and to intuit underlying organisational patterns which are relevant to the consultant(s).

The degree to which the supervisor picks up and amplifies or reduces these relational and emotional patterns depends on both his personal valency and the valencies of his supervisees (Bion 1961). Valency is a term that refers to our individual susceptibility to resonate with various unconscious demands. Bion suggests that human beings have different propensities for responding to, and connecting with, different group emotional patterns. The propensities depend on our own background and personality, both in terms of life experience and experiences at work. Patterns we are able to pick up consciously are patterns that we can recognise and do not overly disturb us. Patterns we tend to pick up unconsciously are patterns that somehow 'stir' us up, unsettle or disturb us, even though we are (not yet) able to identify them or understand them consciously. These patterns leave behind a sort of vague apprehension, a slight frustration or irritation, and often nothing more than that. We can still use them in supervision, provided we are able to become conscious of our own vague feelings and relate them to what happens during a supervision session. The patterns we pick up consciously are related to our life experience, while the patterns we pick up unconsciously are often related to areas of our lives that we haven't really got to grips with and where we feel sensitised, vulnerable or wounded. The fact that they remain unconscious gives an indication that they touch a nerve and that we protect ourselves from them by not observing them too closely. The method by which we do this is the defence mechanism of displacement.

Time after time, supervisors are able to pick up important aspects of consulting, aspects that are normally below the level of conscious awareness, thanks to the reinforcement that takes place during supervision sessions. These aspects include resistance to change, or cultural norms that facilitate or hinder change. But they can pick up these aspects only within a specific and limited range, determined by both the valencies of the supervisees and those of the supervisor himself. This phenomenon is comparable to the phenomenon of 'resonance' in physics where, for example, an antenna can pick up very weak signals but only within a limited range of frequencies. Signals outside that range are not picked up. Different supervisors are therefore likely to pick up different aspects. In addition, they can't help distorting what they pick up. It is therefore important to adopt an open attitude towards all possible impressions, and to continue exploring how relevant the findings are to the supervisee and the client organisation. However striking the findings may appear, let's not forget that supervisor and supervisee are only human and have limited access to the full consulting context.

Each of the contracts or forms of organisation supervision discussed in the previous section offers a different potential for picking up organisational patterns. The organisation consultants act as 'lenses' in terms of picking up and amplifying patterns. The supervisor acts as 'photographic material' that will be affected by specific patterns, emotions and reflections. This is not the full picture, of course, because the 'lenses' (supervisees) themselves are also affected by the material. They pick up patterns just as well, and so they also act as photographic material. Conversely, the supervisor also works as a lens, namely as a lens on the supervisory relationship itself.

Let us take another look at all the different forms of organisation supervision, using the relational ring model that we discussed in Chapter 1 (see Figure 1.1, p. 12).

In *coaching supervision* (see Figure 4.1) the situation is most straightforward, because the supervisor has only one 'lens' (the supervisee) and no direct access to the client organisations that are being discussed. This offers a clear-cut window onto the coaching relationship and behind that the organisational patterns. There is room for amplification and resonance between the two essential relationships of which the coach forms part: the coaching relationship and the supervisory relationship.

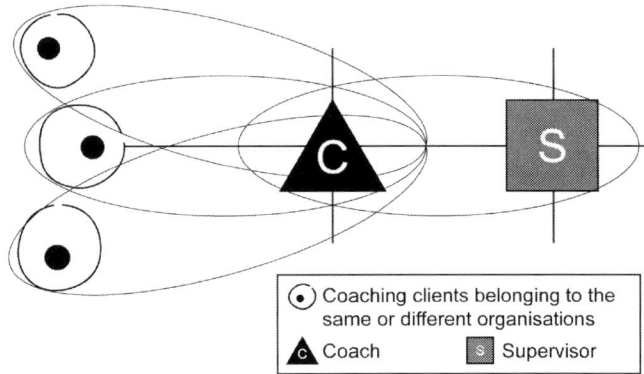

Figure 4.1 Schematic depiction of the relationships within coaching supervision for one individual coach. The vertical lines represent other client–supervisee relationships of the coach and supervisor. The horizontal line to the right of the supervisor connects to *his* supervisor.

In *organisation consulting supervision* there is more room for picking up patterns, as the consultant has been directly exposed to organisational dynamics between people working for the same organisation. The consultant has a broader, more participative role in the client organisation. In a variety of relationships, there is an opportunity to resonate with more valencies. Figure 4.2 illustrates the broader influx of information in the larger number of rings or relationships to which the consultant is exposed. The consultant somehow becomes more 'native' or 'immersed' in the organisation, albeit temporarily, with all of the attendant consequences in terms of relationships.

In *shadow consulting* (see Figure 4.3), the supervisor has access to an even richer dynamic, which can now include the patterns between supervisees as well. He also has more 'antennae' for picking up patterns from the organisation (the supervisees). The relational patterns between consultants are now visible during supervision. These

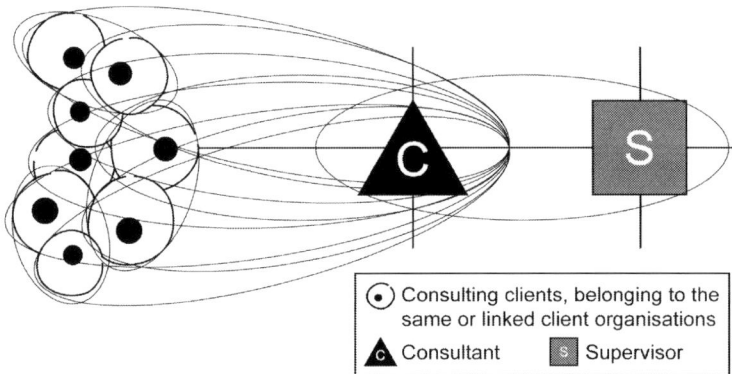

Figure 4.2 Schematic depiction of the relationships within organisation consulting supervision for one individual consultant. The vertical lines represent other client–supervisee relationships of the consultant and supervisor. The horizontal line to the right of the supervisor connects to *his* supervisor.

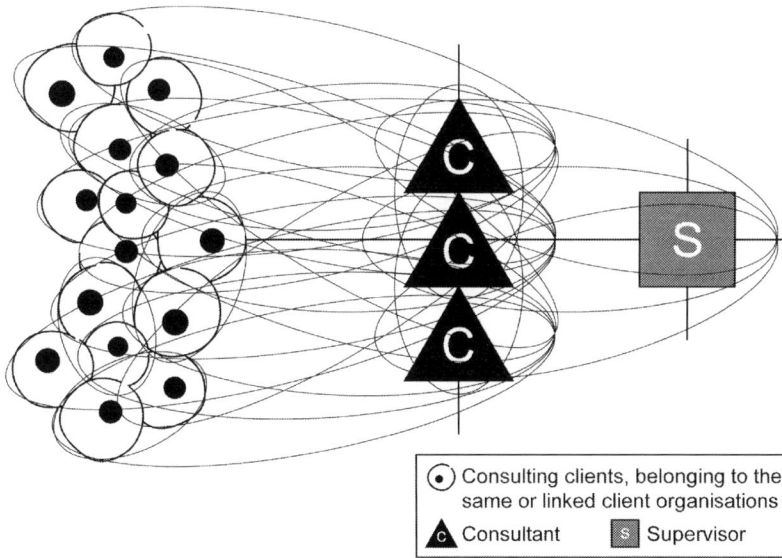

Figure with legend:

(•) Consulting clients, belonging to the same or linked client organisations

△C Consultant   ▪S Supervisor

Figure 4.3 Schematic depiction of the relationships within shadow consulting supervision for a team of consultants working on a single assignment. The vertical lines represent other client–supervisee relationships of the consultants and supervisor. The horizontal line to the right of the supervisor connects to *his* supervisor.

patterns can be influenced by parallel processes and can therefore reflect and mirror organisational patterns. As a result, the supervisor can sometimes observe certain relational patterns directly, as we saw in the examples in the previous section. Another striking example is Hirschhorn's case of a deputy director who is under intense pressure and works with a pair of organisation consultants who are in turn supervised by the author (Hirschhorn 1988: 40).

Finally, in *peer supervision* (see Figure 4.4), the supervisor has access to a still wider spectrum of experience, including his own direct experience with the client organisation. This situation may be richer than that in shadow consulting, but it is also 'messier', as the supervisor will be less clear about what the patterns he is picking up relate to. They may be (unconsciously) prejudged by his own experiences in the organisation and with the consultants' clients. The observations of the peer supervisor are bound to be coloured by his own experience in the organisation, which makes attribution more difficult. External supervision for the peer supervisor becomes more important in our view. This external supervision is a way of testing his own observations and impressions, and of bringing patterns to the surface that had been invisible due to his own immersion in the consulting assignment.

As we can see from Figures 4.2, 4.3 and 4.4, the patterns to which the organisation consulting supervisor is exposed are sometimes four layers deep:

1   Patterns between employees in the organisation;
2   which are passed on to organisation consultants;

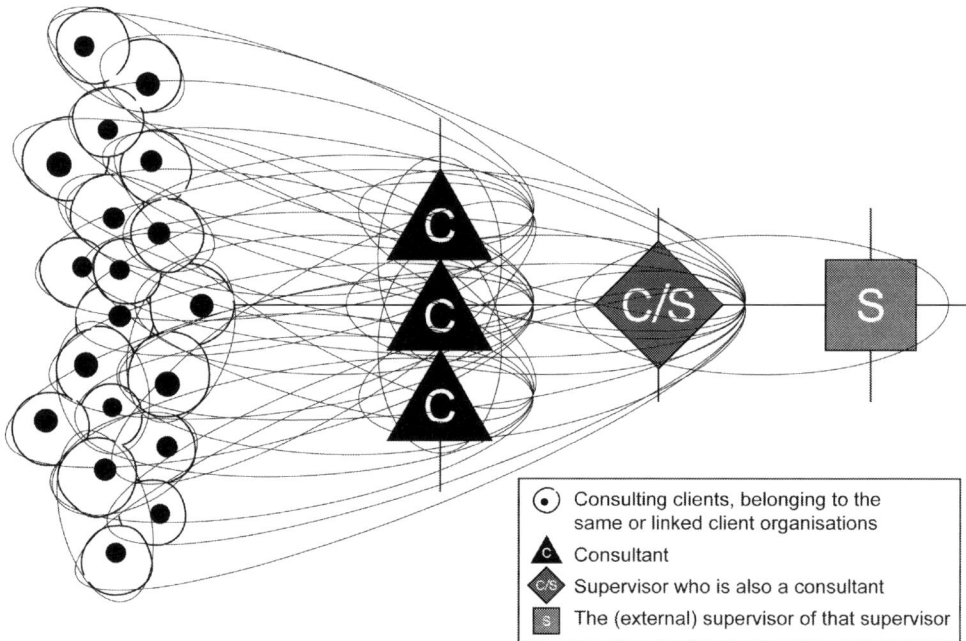

Figure 4.4 Schematic depiction of the relationships within peer supervision for a team of consultants working on a single assignment. The vertical lines represent other client–supervisee relationships of the consultants and supervisor. This time, the supervisor of the peer supervisor is also depicted, because this is the first supervisor who actually stands outside the network and the dynamics of the assignment.

    3   who in turn develop patterns between themselves, partly influenced by what they have experienced in the organisation (because that is the frame of reference they share at present);

    4   who pass these patterns on in turn to the supervisor when they present themselves for supervision.

Distortions can occur from layer to layer due to the highly personal valencies of those involved. Only if space is explicitly reserved for reflection (and sometimes this only happens for the first time during supervision) can these patterns be picked up for conscious processing. It is useful for the supervisor to remain aware that, despite all their experience and the safe and confidential atmosphere of the supervision room, the patterns are still coloured by invisible valencies and unprocessed experiences.

Dilemmas for organisation supervisors

Although the different supervision contracts (coaching supervision, organisation consulting supervision, shadow consulting and peer supervision) are quite distinct from one another, the choices and approaches available to the supervisor are broadly similar. Organisation supervisors are frequently faced with a series of dilemmas which crop up again and again with different supervisees. In this section we give a summary of the main dilemmas we have encountered.

In the first place, as supervisors we feel the limits – and hidden promises – of our valencies quite acutely. We notice the consequences of our own counter-transference (Ledford 1985) without necessarily knowing what it is about. We feel unease, irritation, desire, distraction, frustration, boredom or other feelings that feel authentic but do not stem only from ourselves. These barely perceptible feelings that were initially triggered by the case material can oppress and constrain us, as long as they remain unrelated to the case material. In other words, we start out by feeling sensations in our 'antennae' before we can even begin to make sense of the signal. Only by attending to the irritation itself and to our impressions in this moment can we hope to receive a clearer signal. But as we do that, we also become aware of the problems with our perception, the fallibility of our 'measuring equipment', because we notice the extent to which the receiving of the signals is bound up with our mood at the time and our own unprocessed material that is stirred up. The dilemma begins as a discomfort and then develops into a choice of whether or not to attend to the impressions and signals. We sometimes experience deep doubts as to whether, and to what extent, this internal 'carry-on' can be relevant to our supervisee(s). Organisation supervision complicates the level of self-awareness – i.e., listening to the self (as discussed in Chapter 2) or the sixth 'eye' in terms of the seven-eyed model (adapted to consulting supervision by Hawkins and Smith 2006): small hunches or vague feelings can have deep significance for the organisational work and there is less room for checking these hunches directly.

The second dilemma opens up when we start to communicate our observations: how forcefully are we going to do that? And how much room for doubt do we want to leave? Often, what works best is to communicate both: both conviction, with sharp, concise and bold observations, and room for doubt, with an invitation for further reflection.

The third dilemma is related to this and has to do with who is leading the conversation. This is a well-known consultant's dilemma around leading and following, or whether or not to be directive. Is it more useful for the supervisor to facilitate, similar to the way a consultant or coach might work? Or is it important to be more directive with our observations and to map the various aspects of the case more actively, working more like an expert or mentor?

We experience similar dilemmas in relation to the style of supervision, facing a choice between a reflective, more cerebral way of working in sessions and a more 'playful' approach – for example, by recreating the organisation's dynamics in the form of role-play, psychodrama or organisation constellations (de Haan 2004). Such role-plays can provide more direct access to unconscious patterns in the client organisation by, in a sense, circumventing self-censure and other obstacles to transference.

Other dilemmas have more to do with the role that we play for the client organisation – i.e. for those who will ultimately reap the benefits of supervision. The organisation of the supervisee's clients is the 'ultimate client', even though these clients are usually one step removed from the supervision itself and as a result have no direct experience or knowledge of the supervision sessions. Due to this indirect link, supervisors will struggle somewhat with their role for the organisation, or forget that they have a role in and for the client organisation. Moreover, just as for consultants, there is the dilemma between on the one hand being too detached and not really picking up the organisational patterns, and on the other hand being too closely engaged and thus having a direct involvement in the client organisation, an involvement that generally goes wrong because the supervisor has not entered into an explicit and agreed contract with the client organisation.

The image that sometimes arises is that of the supervisor as a documentary film-maker. The supervisor is present mainly in an observing capacity and goes unnoticed by the 'wildlife' in the organisation. But as the budgets grow and the film-maker is present more often in an ecosystem which is unfolding before his lens, a negative impact on the biotope becomes inevitable. The scrutinising lenses of organisation supervisors are not just passively observing, they are also – and generally more than we think – meaningful 'objects' in the field of view of the people in the organisation. In addition, they may unintentionally become a yardstick for them in measuring developments in the organisation. If this risk exists, supervisors are well advised to conclude a carefully worded agreement with the organisation itself.

Finally, we have also experienced dilemmas concerning the normative aspect of supervision, the fact that the supervisor acts as a 'gatekeeper' for the supervisee. It is often the case that a manager of external consultants will adopt a style where he leaves the consultant(s) to their own devices as far as possible and is primarily interested in billable days. Consultants often contribute to this division of labour, because they are generally keen to operate as freely as possible. This often means that the most meaningful conversations that the consultant has about his own performance and the development of his own consulting practice are those with his supervisor. But it also means that the supervisor runs the risk of stepping into the manager's shoes, of becoming a sort of 'co-manager' of the consultant.

Some consultancy firms have a system of internal 'mentors' to help the supervisor and manager with this aspect of performance management. The mentor can hold regular conversations with the consultant that go beyond billable days and other practical matters.

CASE EXAMPLE: MENTORING AND ORGANISATION-CONSULTING SUPERVISION

Jules was a recent recruit who had joined a medium-sized change consultancy. Her background had been in local government, where she had been responsible for organisation development and had managed a sizeable budget for change, training and development within the organisation. On joining the organisation, she was assigned an internal 'mentor' who would support her as she made the transition from 'internal' to 'external' consultant.

During her first assignment, in another local authority, Jules found that she was taken much more seriously by senior management in the organisation than she had been by her previous colleagues. This was both enjoyable and worrying at the same time. Enjoyable because she felt more influential and that people really listened to her. Worrying because she was not familiar with the new context and way of working. She was afraid that her clients would act on her advice and might get into difficulties, and that it would be her fault in some way.

Her internal mentor, an experienced supervisor, suggested that Jules start attending the peer supervision sessions held once a month at the client site, as she suspected that part of Jules' uneasiness was due to a parallel process, a form of co-dependence. The internal mentor enquired about what Jules learned from the supervision meetings and found that they did indeed talk regularly about the risk of making clients unnecessarily dependent on their consultant. Meanwhile she helped Jules reflect on her transition and her expectations – for example, concerning what 'good performance' meant to her in her first year.

The combination of peer supervision and internal mentoring was effective and Jules quickly learned how to value her own expertise and experience while remaining curious about her new role and what she could learn in the consultancy. Her mentor also coached her in working in a less directive way and facilitating her client's thinking process more than she was used to doing.

Organisation supervision is an exciting, ever-changing field where there is still a lot of scope for development. Our prediction is that, as our knowledge increases and our methodology improves, we will be better placed to help organisation consultants and others, such as experts, coaches, process facilitators and interim managers, more effectively handle their valencies, the boundaries around their assignments and the parallel processes that will inevitably develop between themselves and their organisational clients.

Summary

Consultants work as outsiders within client organisations and run all sorts of risks as a result, such as, on the one hand, the risk of operating with too much detachment and so failing to offer any actual help, and, on the other hand, the risk of becoming too involved and thus absorbed into their client system. Supervision helps them, in case after case, to find their own personal balance between these and other polarities.

Consultants and supervisors can work together in three different contracts:

- **Individual supervision of consultants:** focuses mainly on what is going on for the consultant and is ideal as a form of quality assurance for the consulting practice.
- **Shadow consulting as a form of organisation supervision:** focuses mainly on what is going on in the organisation and is ideal for picking up invisible but motivating patterns in organisations.

- **Peer supervision within consulting teams:** focuses mainly on peer support and picks up rich patterns, but doesn't always know how to attribute them.

Each of these contracts has its pros and cons. In the first two forms, the supervisor can pick up many more organisational patterns and consulting relationships and discuss them freely. In the last form, the supervisor has his own direct experience of the client organisation and therefore works more as an internal consultant to the consultants.

Picking up phenomena within the consulting relationships and within client organisations starts at an unconscious level. The role of the supervisor in the first instance is to pick up barely perceptible patterns, emotions and impulses within himself. To do this, the supervisor uses his own counter-transference – or, to be precise, his own **valencies**. Valency is a highly personal way of co-resonating with the supervisee and of participating in the anxieties, forces and conflicts to which the supervisee is exposed. In so doing, the supervisor cannot avoid being affected by these phenomena himself. Valency for an organisation supervisor is therefore a relational phenomenon which is closely connected with his specific countertransference.

Dilemmas that organisation supervisors experience in their work include the following.

- Working with counter-transference means working with one's own unconscious, unprocessed patterns. What part of this comes from me? What comes from my supervisee? And what comes from the client organisation? Counter-transference remains an unreliable guide, precisely because it is so raw and undigested and will remain unprocessed to a certain extent.
- The dilemma between being impactful and tentative. The art of putting forward a hypothesis convincingly and at the same time so carefully that it invites exploratory reflection.
- The dilemma between following and leading: unfolding the issue and leading the exploration.
- The dilemma between reflection and role-play.
- The dilemma between aloofness and involvement, or between abstinence and collusion.
- The dilemma between normative interventions (monitoring boundaries) and stepping into the shoes of the assignment leader or the consultant's manager.

5 Transcript of a supervision session: all the things I didn't say

with Elaine Robinson

Here is a transcript of a real-life supervision session that we have made anonymous for publication. In our view, it illustrates how supervision is different from coaching, consulting, mentoring and other forms of 'helping' conversations.

This transcript illustrates how it often feels to be 'in supervision'. Among other things, it highlights the common tantalising experience of discovering new points of view, of gathering ideas to help our client, when it is essentially too late. Supervision makes us think about the myriad things that we did not say to our client, the many things that we were not even aware of. Supervision helps us to generate the right

SUPERVISION AS...
Tantalus with an esprit de l'escalier

response in a difficult consulting situation, precisely when it is too late and the moment has passed. Nevertheless, we think that this fragment of supervision also demonstrates how a consultant or coach can gain fresh perspectives during supervision which are vitally important for future coaching work or follow-up sessions with the same client.

The text from this point until the 'Postscript' section is Elaine's.

Hidden treasures in the gestures of coach and client

I have been coaching Justin since November. It is now May and we have just had our final session. Justin's main agenda with the coaching was to progress his career within the organisation, a manufacturing company based in Basildon. In fact he has recently been made commercial director of a large branch of the company. A few days after my final session with Justin I had my fourth supervision session with Erik. I had prepared a list of three items, as follows:

1   I was struck and delighted by the changes Justin said he had made during the coaching period which made me think the coaching had been worthwhile for him. For example, he was now delegating more, he had arranged one-to-ones with his team and he had approached his boss about promotion; all new behaviours directly attributable to our sessions.

2   However, I felt disappointment that despite the positive things Justin said about how much he'd achieved, and the fact that he'd 'ticked all the boxes' relating to his experience with a resounding 'yes', I had inwardly also hoped he would write down some positive evaluative comments on the feedback form but he did not. Part of this desire I admit was to receive positive validation about my coaching, even though I know this should not be a prime concern of a coach. Moreover, positive comments are helpful for commercial reasons, testimony for future clients and so on.

3   Finally, I was struck by the fact that he'd brought a presentation he'd prepared and wanted to talk me through. I found this unusual and wondered if Justin wanted to impress me.

These three points became the basis for our supervision discussion. I was pleased I had prepared because one of my underlying worries was that frequently coaching sessions seem to go so well I wonder whether I'll ever have any 'issues' to discuss with my supervisor. How wrong could I be?

I had several coaching sessions with Erik before he became my coaching supervisor, so we had already built rapport and a good relationship. I explained to Erik that there are still places I 'don't go to' with my coachees, most probably because I'm fearful of being unkind or hurtful. For example, I had previously seen Justin give another presentation at Basildon. My main reflection during that presentation was, 'He looks too casual, doesn't cut a figure of seniority, he needs to get off the windowsill and take his hands out of his pockets.' Yet when he asked me directly what I'd thought about his presentation I had to stop myself just saying, 'Fine, you were great.' I think what I actually said was, in a typical coaching style, 'How did you think it went?' In retrospect that seems a bit like a coaching cop-out. I also said it had been a good team effort, which was true, but I still did not get to the heart of what would have been authentic feedback.

A repeated pattern is that when I ask Erik about the things I use as tools and props, he says he rarely uses any such thing. This was also the case with Erik's own evaluation form (similar to the review form discussed on p. 117) that he kindly sent me afterwards to compare with mine. He has one but then often chooses not to use it. He said this was probably because clients often don't bother to send it back anyway, and he wouldn't want to leave them with that slight sense of guilt of not having completed the form. I agreed with him that his form is more likely to generate commentary and insight for the coachee and feedback for the coach. Erik's background, style and the extent of his experience means he is more likely to discard a theory, model or form than use it. My coaching form was easy to complete and invited a 'tick box' approach, and I saw Erik's as probably more of a 'blank page'. I commented that our form relates partly to our processes but Erik made the point that asking these questions of the coachee at the end of the session could signal that I am not sure about the quality of my offering. Plus, it makes me self-conscious. I had never thought of that. We both observed that being self-conscious to what others think of me has been a theme that emerges in my supervisory sessions.

Erik then launched into some great supervision questions. 'How much feedback do you want in the interests of your coaching practice, and how much does client feedback then influence you? Who are you doing this for? (e.g. your client, your future business, or your own confidence?)'

On the point of Justin's presentation, Erik asked whether I thought Justin may be trying to obtain some fresh thinking that he could use. Or could it be in a sense to present to the teacher or even to show off? If so, what would you want your response to be? What is the gesture of your client? And could there be hidden treasures in the gesture for you to work on?

Once Erik starts using delicious words like 'gestures' and 'treasures' I nearly miss the point, but Erik quickly brings me back saying, 'Do you experience this as hoping to improve the presentation or in some way as asking for "strokes" in a similar way you were with your feedback form?'

A parallel process in this session?

He then added his own commentary: 'How about this session, between you and me? You seem to present your vulnerabilities quite easily and I wonder whether that is also a gesture of inviting in fresh thinking?' Erik notices my vulnerability but he also helpfully guides me: 'Showing a presentation is not a straightforward request, and would it be possible to talk about the request itself, rather than just attending to it?'

In relation to Justin's presentation at his workplace, had I expressed myself directly to Justin I would have said something like, 'You need to smarten your act up.' Erik suggested, quite reasonably, that although there may be risk in saying such a thing and some skill required in saying it in a non-judgemental way, this may also be offering up a treasure; something Justin wouldn't have heard otherwise or from anyone else. Others may have the same thought about Justin's presentations.

Now my feelings are I wish I had said that to him, it doesn't seem such an outrageous thing to say after all, although I would say it in the full recognition that there is risk and that in terms of my coaching practice anything I say should have Justin's interests foremost.

Erik wondered if my avoidance of direct feedback to Justin was partly out of compassion for him or even compassion for myself. When I suggested that perhaps I could go back to Justin or send him a message with some of the things I'd learned during supervision, Erik said that I was experiencing something the French call *l'esprit de l'escalier*. It is the classic feeling of diplomats and civil servants who come out of one of the *grands hôtels particuliers* after a tense, senior meeting and then – typically on the stairs on their way out – suddenly realise what they 'should' have answered. It was first used by Diderot in *Paradoxe sur le Comédien* and captures well the experience of thinking of a clever comeback when it is too late. The phenomenon is usually accompanied by a feeling of regret at not having thought of the approriate response when it was most needed or suitable. This makes supervision feel like the vexations of Tantalus: you see all this wonderful nurture hanging around but when you reach out for it the realisation that it comes too late for nourishing the client blows it away.

Erik said that he noticed some patterns such as the interest of Justin and me in feedback, confirmation and reassurance all at the same time. Erik saw this as potentially rich. I just have to ask myself 'Why?' Why is validation or positive evaluation of me by others important to me? Why so important in this case? Erik pursued his theme and wondered if the issues of the client were resonating with me, and asked me to think about whether I and my client had any themes or patterns in common.

For example, what feeds Justin's drive to go to the next level in his role? I mentioned the relationship between Justin and his brother as a possible explanation. I had previously mentioned that Justin comes from a high-flying professional family of lawyers. Erik thought Justin seemed paralysed by some of the suggestions of his boss. So Erik asked, is there a parallel between Justin's situation and my own? I had not consciously thought of this possibility at all, but when it was put to me so directly I realised there were certain parallels. Still more *l'esprit de l'escalier* on my part.

I did notice resonance within myself of the kind Erik had suggested, such as a degree of envy of Justin's glamorous world and the multi-million deals he makes around the globe. I recognised Justin's ambition to step up and achieve the next level, and I realised I could only be fully on Justin's side when I am aware of these patterns within myself. There was a realisation that I could have said to Justin something like, 'You're in sales, why don't you sell yourself?' Again, I was left wishing, 'Why didn't I say that at the time?' Or would that be too harsh a challenge?

Erik said that all these regrets, doubts and fears of a coach need to be managed somehow. That would help us in our work, even if it doesn't contribute to a session that lies in the past. This is why we need supervision not just to be a better coach, but also to stay in touch with our present emotion and intuition.

So I then decided to take the bull by the horns. I summoned up my courage and asked Erik a direct question: 'When you give me feedback are you being direct or are you being how I was with Justin and couching things in a certain way so as not to hurt me or be unkind?' Erik thought that a great question on account of the parallels with myself and Justin – which, as I could not help noticing, pleased me. His answer was that he always tries to be frank but then sometimes feels a regret. He said he regretted once using the term 'narcissistic' with me, which just 'bubbled up', and since it is frequently used as a stigmatising label Erik felt troubled afterwards about using it. Actually, I didn't mind at the time and I had some fun reading about it and responding to it in our next session, so it was a treasure for me rather than a risk.

Erik also demonstrated a key distinction between being a coach and a supervisor, because he said if he was still my coach he would probably not answer that direct question but would more likely explore what lay behind it. In supervision he speaks more freely about the profession, and about the choices he makes as a coach or supervisor. That aspect is interesting to me, and it makes me think the supervisee is perhaps considered to be able to 'take it' more than a coachee.

From doubt, to *esprit de l'escalier*, to compassion

We discussed Justin's Schein Career Anchor profile (Schein 1978). Erik expressed curiosity that the Lifestyle anchor was high, perhaps showing that Justin would not be strongly driven to his goal of promotion, and that he may be ambivalent in his motivation for the next level up. Again, why didn't I ask Justin that question?

We talked about the technical side of Justin's business and its division into three separate companies, one concentrating on what he termed the 'bread and butter' and the other two moving into state-of-the-art technologies. I really like using idiomatic expressions like these in my coaching supervision with Erik because being Dutch he responds with great interest to English language idiosyncracies. Justin was to be on the management team of the first company, which was perhaps the less exciting or innovative side of the business. As a consequence he might feel promoted but at the same time denigrated by the modest aspirations of his new division. Erik enabled me to see the irony (or Pyrrhic victory) that Justin could be promoted and still lose – another ground for ambivalence in his ambition to be promoted to the next level. There is not much fun in sales if the only aim is to have a better margin. The sales department could be viewed as being quite weakened in this context. Again, I simply hadn't thought of this.

In a way for me it is both exposing and tantalising to be supervised. I share some of my greatest doubts or concerns regarding my work, and I often hear 'these are understandable concerns' or 'here are some more concerns', so I don't always feel exactly invigorated by how my vulnerabilities are taken up. Very often, as in this session, I feel I should have said different things to my client, my *esprit de l'escalier* plays up and leaves me frustrated about my work. However, I do benefit from supervision in a deeper way. I think afresh, deepen my understanding, and acquire both new metaphors for my work and alternatives for my practice, even if they come too late for using with this particular client in the particular session talked about in supervision.

We spoke about how often I said, 'I hadn't thought of that' in this supervision session. Erik reminded me that this session may not be lost even if none of it flows back to the client. In fact, I could diminish myself in Justin's eyes if I now go back with the things I wished I'd said.

If a client cries or is emotional, it is all right within the safety of the coaching session and makes them stronger to face the outside world. Similarly, if coaches feel inadequate in supervision and they are able to tolerate this feeling, their self-confidence may grow substantially, along with their alternatives for action.

I was reminded that Justin said his next main issue was the 'supply chain' and I recalled to Erik that I was crestfallen as I'd seen this as something quite boring rather than interesting, because I was rather hoping for a 'people' issue. I wondered if Justin had read my face at that moment. Erik perked up again when he heard this: 'For sales, the supply chain is a real and continuous challenge because they make all sorts of promises and agreements and have to wait and see if their colleagues in the chain will deliver on those promises. Their own reputation with the client depends on the quality of, or their influence on, the supply process. You too, Elaine, are in fact part of his "supply process", so perhaps he was talking about you.'

In summary, for me it is interesting just to notice when I feel excited or triggered to work with Justin, and when I feel bored – and how much of that was my agenda, how much of that I had actually picked up from Justin. I can never fully answer that question, but it's fascinating to consider. This helped me to realise how important it is to try and see things from the coachee's perspective first and foremost, but then also to pay attention to my own feelings in response.

Postscript

We believe it is important to emphasise that this experience of *l'esprit de l'escalier*, like that of *déjà vu*, is illusory. We would be foolish to really believe that it is too late, that we can't do anything more to the conversation that we're now looking at from a fresh perspective. The opposite is true: it is *during* that realisation that we alter the conversation that ended just now, or a week ago. Conversations, like relationships, are ongoing processes. They don't start when the 'honourable members' take their places around the table, or finish when they stand up. As long as conversations and relationships continue to exist in the minds and hearts of the participants, they are not dead or finished. A new realisation about a relationship or conversation is, therefore, by definition, a new chapter in that relationship or conversation.

Even now, while writing this chapter, the echoes from conversation to conversation continue: Justin with his presentation, and the mixture of pride and fishing for compliments that drove him, then Elaine with her presentation of her completed evaluation form, again with a mixture of pride and compliment-seeking, and now Elaine and Erik who have written this chapter together and are left with precisely the same feeling of pride because we have created a record of an authentic supervision session, mixed with the hope that readers will appreciate it and see us as friendly, competent professionals. Parallel processes never end: each time a conversation from the past is revisited, the underlying dynamic during that conversation is revisited with it. The result is a recursive process, where every new topic of conversation opens a window through to another conversation, in which the same topic is found to stem from elsewhere, and so on, to ever more archaic, primitive or archetypical precursors, which can be regarded as genealogies of whole families or family trees of conversations.

Learning from supervision needn't always take place in retrospect: it can also take place *beforehand*, with an *esprit* that occurs to us on the stairs as we enter the consulting or coaching conversation rather than as we leave it, as illustrated by the following case example.

CASE EXAMPLE

Executive coach Leanne is aware that she has a supervision session later this week, when she will probably be discussing the client with whom she has an appointment today. During the last four meetings the client has done most of the talking and Leanne was able to intervene only with enormous difficulty. The client says she finds the sessions really helpful, mainly as a 'contemplation' of her busy practice, as she puts it. However, Leanne herself has the impression that all the client is doing is venting her feelings in an unbroken monologue of largely rigid and fixed ideas and that her client is deeply entrenched in her (lack of) reflection. The so-called 'contemplation' doesn't appear to be of much benefit to her so Leanne decides this time to practise with a more active style: she needs to have something to offer her supervisor, after all. If she sits through another whole session without bringing forth much apart from the occasional – and to her mind, disappointing – summary, there won't be anything to talk about on Friday.

Later in the week she does indeed bring this session to supervision. She has worked it out in detail so as to learn from it (classical supervision method, see Chapter 6). The supervision is rather flat and awkward, and it seems as if neither Leanne nor her supervisor can add much to what is already down on paper about the client and the session earlier in the week – until the supervisor suddenly remarks: 'You say that the client talks constantly and that you don't have anything to contribute. But here I read a fair number of things that you have said, especially towards the end of the session, including some pretty sharp turns of phrase it seems to me.' Only then does Leanne say that she wanted to have something to offer during the supervision and not just sit there at a loss for words. They both agree that Leanne has already made a positive change in her client relationship earlier in the week, on the basis of her future supervision session, and that it appears worthwhile to continue with this client in the same vein.

Summary

During supervision we often review recent conversations, asking ourselves if we could look at those conversations and relationships differently.

Elaine looks back **with satisfaction** at a completed course of coaching. Her client has achieved a great deal and made measurable progress. However, she also has some doubts.

Supervision gives her an opportunity to celebrate her **success**, but the focus quickly shifts to her **doubts**. Underlying them is a sense of shame: did she withhold feedback from her client, Justin? Did she plan to use Justin and his positive feedback as a 'business card' to attract future clients? What exactly is the state of her self-confidence? Does it emerge to be somewhat fragile as we continue to ask questions about the coaching?

In the supervision session we discover connections between Justin's attitude towards Elaine, his coach, and Elaine's attitude towards Erik, her supervisor. And we discover a multitude of things that Elaine could have said to Justin, which it is now too late to say. The sheer torment that is *l'esprit de l'escalier* hits home.

Elaine bravely perseveres and continues to look at herself, while contributing new material. In the end she finds enough **compassion** for herself and her client to leave the coaching the way it is, and to forgive herself for her fragile self-confidence and opportunism, aspects which, after all, would be familiar to most coaches in similar circumstances.

After the compassion comes the **realisation** that this session has generated ideas and techniques that can benefit Justin indirectly, and a sense of reassurance with inspiration to treat similar clients in the same way, and at the same time differently, in the future.

All of which can be described as a fairly common outcome and can generally serve as a model for a successful supervision session.

6 Supervision methods: improvisation and structure

SUPERVISION AS...
Two rather frightened people,
finding out the unknown

In a way, providing supervision amounts to nothing more – or less! – than just listening, observing and interpreting (see Chapter 2), all simultaneously. For this reason it cannot really be described as a 'method'. Allowing unprompted observations and discoveries to bubble to the surface is all that is required, together with a healthy dose of conversational technique and relationship maintenance. This makes it hard to think of step-by-step methods and detailed protocols for supervision.

Indeed, where is the evidence to support pre-structured methods or protocols?[1] In my own experience, rather, it is precisely the doubt, the fundamental not

---

[1] See Appendix B for an outline of the evidence we do have. What little there is doesn't look good for supervisors who like protocols and manuals.

knowing what to do, the uncertainty of where to go, the likelihood of failing to grasp the full meaning or even of getting it wrong, that are extremely productive in supervision. To paraphrase Bion (1973/1974): 'In every supervision room there ought to be two rather frightened people; the supervisor and the supervisee. If they are not, one wonders why they are bothering to find out what everyone knows.'[2]

Nevertheless, it does help to have a broad idea about flow and structure for supervisory conversations. Structures will generally be different for individual and group supervision. Here is an overview of simple conversational models that have proved their worth in practice – not to restrict supervision in any way but more in order to illustrate the emphases that experienced supervisors apply in their work.

Working with the past in supervision

Leaving aside rare methodology where the supervisor listens in live to the consultant's work, sometimes being able to communicate with the consultant through an earpiece, a lot of time in supervision is spent reflecting on past client work with the aim of learning from past experiences and improving one's practice. For this kind of reflection the past needs to be registered and recorded, perceived, processed and memorised, so it is worthwhile thinking for a moment about the intricacies of human perception, cognition and memory.

We cannot, and do not, notice everything about our experiences. There are limits to what our perceptual apparatus can notice, so we have to filter or edit what we take in. This was dramatically shown by Simons and Chabris (1999), who made a short film of Harvard students playing basketball. One team is wearing black shirts, the other white. After making the film, they asked volunteers to watch and count how many passes were made by the team in white. Less than a minute after the film finished, they asked viewers if they had noticed anything unusual. Over half said no and had failed to notice a student in a gorilla suit walking into the scene, visible for nine seconds. This research demonstrated how we pay selective attention and in doing so fail to notice other elements. Research has also shown that the information we tend to notice is that which affirms and supports our existing view of the world – what psychologists refer to as the 'confirmation bias' – rather than information or data that challenges beliefs we hold dear. This would suggest that particularly those of us who are consultants and coaches may unconsciously edit out aspects of our client work that do not support our self-image and self-esteem.

I have talked so far about perceptual and cognitive limitations in coding experiences. But what about the processes of recall? Memory traces are ever-changing. They are changed by the experience itself and later by the passing of time (Fivush and Neisser 1994). In fact, memory appears to be essentially a 'social construction' – in other words, a reconstruction of whatever is being remembered, taking into account the circumstances at the time of remembering. It is an active process that creates a new

---

[2] In this quote I replaced 'consulting room' with 'supervision room', 'patient' with 'supervisee' and 'psychoanalyst' with 'supervisor'.

narrative that will bear some resemblance to earlier narratives or to a recording of the same experience. However, memory will also necessarily include new narrative elements, born of emotional and cognitive processes during the passing of time or prevailing at the time of recall. It is well-known that the activity of recounting itself engenders both censorship and new creativity (Goodman *et al.* 2006). This leads to the addition of newly-imagined elements to what is remembered and the deletion of others.

There are a variety of ways in which past experience can be submitted to supervision. At one end of the spectrum, supervisees use free association and storytelling, which give free rein to the reconstructing processes of memory. They will then not only somehow reflect the 'real' experience but just as much the supervisee's processing of that experience, and also the supervisee's emotions and experiences here and now, during the retelling of and reflecting on their experiences. At the other end of the spectrum, supervisees can preserve a more objective trace of the client work that is being recalled for supervision. The supervisee will then bring – for example – the written contract, psychometric information about their clients, or recordings of sessions. This is a fundamentally different way of working in supervision, which allows the supervision process to revisit some aspects of the original event, in undistorted form. Obviously, however good the recording, many other aspects related to mood, atmosphere and non-verbal communication will still be lost and a large part of the work of supervision will still centre around establishing a new, subjective 'truth' of the experience.

In fact we can picture supervision methods on a scale that ranges from extemporisation to objective recording.

1 (*Memory trace*) Free storytelling, where the supervisee is not encouraged to prepare for the session, but rather extemporises his account of client experience. There is a risk that the supervisee may censor, suppress or hold back key elements of his experience. On the other hand the supervisee will also convey how the event has been processed up until this session, so there is a good opportunity for noticing the supervisee's emotions and intentions with the client work.

2 (*Memory captured*) The supervisee writes an account that is as faithful and complete as possible, immediately after the consulting work or session that he wishes to bring to supervision (as in the classical supervision method – see p. 99). Such a written account reflects the early processing by the supervisee, with interesting lapses of memory and restructuring. An indication of how much processing has already happened immediately after a session is that all of the words spoken in a one-hour session amount to at least 25 full pages of writing, while a written account of such a session does not exceed four pages even if memory is still very vivid and reliable.

3 (*Recorded trace*) The supervisee brings a recording or a transcription of a recording (or both) to the supervision session. Now we have the actual words spoken and, in the case of a recording, also a lot of non-verbal information unaffected by memory or the passing of time. We have a 'literal' trace of the session and this can be contrasted and compared with the supervisee's

experience of the session. There is now ample opportunity for surprising the supervisee with new observations and original material which was initially completely missed.

I think that while during supervision the supervisee busies himself with memory and a desire to learn and improve, the supervisor best approaches the session 'without memory and desire', to quote another of Bion's famous encouragements (1970). It is best for the supervisor to stay in the moment and to notice content, affect and parallel process right now, without being distracted by a past event or by hopes for the future.

There are a number of ethical considerations when using transcripts or tapes in supervision. When using recall or transcript notes to share a case with their supervisor, supervisees should be asked to edit out identifying details about the client such as their name or where they work. Such minor edits efficiently preserve anonymity. However, as soon as we use audio the client's voice is present and their first name is likely to be used in the recording, so confidentiality becomes paramount and it is best for supervisor and supervisee to delete the recording straight after supervision.

In my experience, the choice about whom to ask to audio-tape is a sensitive one in the first place. In certain industries, such as audit, investment banking or social services, where litigation and regulation feature prominently, clients may feel constrained by their work context from being taped. In some post-totalitarian countries clients have deeply rooted cultural fears of using any tools which evoke memories of 'surveillance'. So, in addition to anticipating sensitivities, the supervisor can help the supervisee to contract clearly with the client they would like to tape. It is good practice to get written consent beforehand.

In contracting, it is important to emphasise that the audio tape is for the supervisee's benefit and learning so that the focus of the supervisor's attention will be on the coach or consultant as much as on the client. This may help address underlying anxieties the client may have about needing to perform and be the 'good client', or appearing silly to some imagined highly expert supervisor. And of course, it is also vital that the coach makes it explicit that the client can say 'no, thank you' to being taped. However, I have found that in many cases, the very fact that the consultant discloses his own need and desire to learn and asks for the client's help in this endeavour by allowing the session to be taped, can actually herald a deeper level of trust between coach and client, as it may redefine the relationship towards one of mutual needs.

In terms of equipment I would recommend using a phone with a recording function or a small digital voice recorder, as these devices are unobtrusive and it is now normal to have a smart-phone or similar on the table in front of us. Smart-phones are easy to use, and equally easy to misuse. Data can be lost or accidentally transferred. So, supervisees need to be really careful in handling these files and adjusting their settings to prevent data floating across the ether. Once the audio tape has been made, a copy should, out of courtesy, be offered to clients. However, in my experience they rarely take this opportunity. On occasions when a client does ask for a copy, there is some risk of a backlash as clients may find they sound less coherent than expected or develop other concerns.

An audio recording is digital information that can be transmitted, mislaid and misdirected much more easily than conventional notes. The supervisee needs to ensure that any file is protected via secure passwords. In addition the supervisor and supervisee need to delete all the versions of the audio file after its use, and need to inform the client of this in advance.

Working with written transcripts is more straightforward as it is best *not* to ask clients for permission as this may have major and unnecessary impact on the consulting or coaching relationship: the client may express a wish to read the transcript, and may be seriously distracted and even feel imposed upon when seeing the selection and wording that the supervisee has chosen to write up the session. Written transcripts are best kept in anonymous form, away from the client, in a safe place, and for a limited time.

Working with the future in supervision

Interestingly, there are similar dilemmas for supervisor and supervisee when it comes to working with the future. Again, one can opt for a 'literal' form of preparing for the future, or else one can choose a much more 'associative' relationship with future change and preparation for future client work. Here is a similar overview with three options covering the full range of possibilities:

1. (*Reflection trace*) The supervision session is reflective in nature and leads to new perspectives, new insight and new ideas for the future. It is left to the supervisee to translate these reflections into new action. There is a risk of the process becoming cerebral and stilted. On the other hand, there is ample opportunity for generating new insight and overcoming obstacles to growth and development.
2. (*Reflection captured*) The supervision session, although mainly reflective, leads to an action plan or a specific, agreed intention to change something in the supervisee's practice. The reflections are captured during or just after supervision, to generate commitment to future action.
3. (*Rehearsed trace*) The supervision itself is a foreshadowing of the future, with the help of experimentation. The supervisee engages in coaching or consulting during supervision – in other words, he tries out new approaches to clients here and now with the supervisor. Role-play, psychodrama and organisational constellations (de Haan 2004) are examples of this way of working. Even role-playing a past event, while being an associative memory trace, is also an experiment with new action and behaviour, particularly as new versions are tried out. There is a risk that supervision may become entirely behavioural and miss important aspects of the underlying dynamic between supervisee and clients. On the other hand, there is ample opportunity for lively and realistic preparation for the future. Rehearsing future work is particularly rich in group supervision where different colleagues will have different views and feedback. Figure 6.1 shows how these different ways of dealing with past and future in supervision open up different approaches to supervisory conversations.

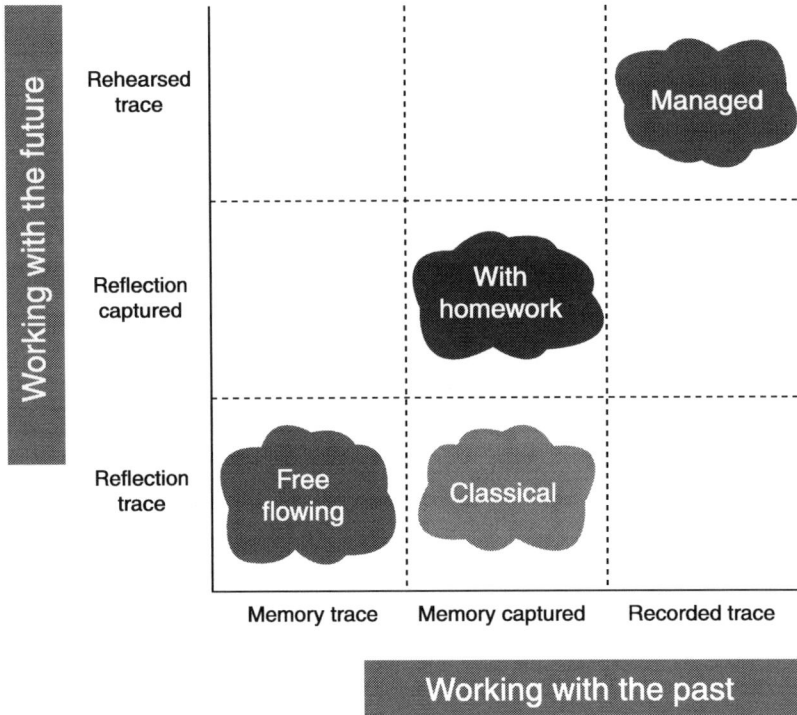

Figure 6.1 How different ways of working with the past and the future can open up different approaches to supervision, including those that are managed in a lot of detail, classical approaches which are based on a detailed summary of consulting or coaching sessions, supervision that leads to 'homework' for the supervisee, and much more free-flowing approaches.

Working with groups and individuals

It is advisable to limit the size of groups for group supervision to between three and eight. Supervision in a group, especially a largish group, needs to be managed fairly tightly to generate the maximum number of relevant observations and perspectives from all group members within a limited space of time. In addition, it is important to steer the session away from questions and initial observations towards deeper interpretations, and to claim time for ourselves as supervisors and our own insights. Due to the customary convergent group dynamic (see Asch 1951), what often happens is that the group unconsciously comes to a consensus fairly quickly on a particular case. It is then up to the supervisor to break through this 'groupthink' and contrast other perspectives with those of the group. Especially where ethical issues are under discussion, it often takes a degree of courage on the supervisor's part to draw attention to something the rest of the group is ignoring for the sake of convenience.

CASE EXAMPLE: GROUP SUPERVISION

This is the third meeting of a supervision group that is due to meet five times in principle. Romilly is an internal coach with a major telecoms provider. She brings the case of her client Adam, who was recently appointed manager of a financial department and has a background as an engineer in the company. She pours out her initial impressions and immediate preconceptions of Adam (as being rather distant, impersonal, and having doubts about the benefit of coaching – i.e. as someone who has simply been 'sent' by his boss) and describes her last session with him, in which he unexpectedly burst into a long monologue about how uncomfortable he often feels about managing his staff.

In the first 20-minute supervision session (using the group consultation method – see p. 101), Romilly is assisted by Jane. Romilly describes how, in that last session with Adam, when the coaching unexpectedly took a 'serious' turn, she herself clammed up tight. She suddenly felt insecure and found herself swamped, so to speak, under all the information. She became very cautious and started to beat around the bush for fear of opening up a 'Pandora's box' in Adam, releasing even more emotions. As she recounted the session she stumbled a little over her words and said 'He came into me' rather than 'He came into the room'. Some of those present later described this as a Freudian slip.

What was interesting about discussing the session with Jane, and is fairly typical of group supervision, was that the conversation between Romilly and Jane began to show characteristics of the recent session between Adam and Romilly. Jane initially pursued a line of questioning about the session with Adam, and the same tension developed between Romilly's feelings and the 'safe', 'businesslike' interventions on Jane's part. After a while Jane began to reassure Romilly about what she had done in her session with Adam: 'Perhaps that was exactly the right response in that situation' and 'It sounds as if it really was a helpful session for Adam'. At the end of the session with Romilly, Jane asks her, 'How helpful has this session been for you?' Romilly answers favourably but does say that, 'If we'd had more time you could have asked more questions about my feelings.'

As she comes out from her session with Romilly, Jane says: 'I wasn't sure if I could keep on asking about her feelings. I felt under the pressure of time and tried to achieve a positive outcome within the time available. I felt protective towards Romilly.'

The group then has time to talk further about the session they have just witnessed and about the parallels between Romilly's feelings now and Adam's possible feelings then, and between Jane's feelings now and Romilly's feelings then.[3] Romilly later confirms that she recognises the following feelings on Jane's part from her own situation with Adam: empathy with a client who comes across as rather stern and self-critical; panic about the approaching time-limit (it being the final session with Adam); an inability to contain and process all the emotions released; and confusion due to an overabundance of information, resulting in a protective, complimentary and safe session in which Romilly's questions now, and Adam's questions then, are no longer really the central focus.

Despite the unsatisfactory end to the session between Jane and Romilly, the open discussion of Jane's and Romilly's feelings during that brief consultation session turns

---

[3] An ordinary parallel process, according to the definition in Chapter 2.

out very productive, both for Jane and for Romilly. It also gets the other group members thinking – for example, about the importance of giving full summaries that include sensitive aspects, and establishing an 'informal contract' at the start of any coaching or supervision session.

Romilly goes away with all sorts of ideas about what might have been going on for Adam. She decides not to wait and see if Adam takes up the extra hour of coaching that was included as an option in their contract, but to recommend that he uses it. When Romilly and Adam get together again, they decide to enter into a new contract for four sessions, focusing much more on Adam's feelings and development as a manager and his struggle to lead others in a more personal and less anxious way.

After Romilly the supervision group looks at two more cases. In the next sessions it is clear that the coaches have learned from Jane's grappling with Romilly. They go more smoothly, although not without the emergence of other relevant parallel processes.

Provided the session is tightly managed, it is entirely possible to offer four supervisees a solid supervision session within the space of around three hours, and to make sure all group members are actively involved in these mini supervision sessions. With the group consultation method, therefore, three hours is enough time, based on one group of eight people, for four consultants to contribute case material and four other participants to complete an individual consultation session and receive brief but targeted personal feedback on their coaching skills (see p. 101). Larger groups are sometimes used in training contexts, but make it difficult to keep all of the participants engaged and to avoid the feel of a 'masterclass' or demonstration.

In individual supervision, by contrast, it is important to relinquish leadership of the session itself and, after a brief run-through of the case material to be presented today, to give the session free rein and encourage the supervisee to contribute experiences at his own pace. The supervisor stays silent or 'hums and haws', often for extended periods, to allow the supervisee to associate freely around the subject matter, and steps in only after some 10 or 15 minutes, with summaries, questions or observations of his own. It can also be very positive if the supervisee decides later on in the session to share material that was not divulged at the outset. Such material is often relevant precisely because some initial restraint or shame has been overcome.

For individual supervision I normally assume around 6 to 12 sessions a year, depending on the size of the supervisee's practice. A session usually lasts two hours. A supervisee with a normal consultancy and/or coaching practice will easily find three clients he wants to talk about. In addition, supervision generally involves themes that recur session after session, such as developing assertiveness on the part of clients, or developing a more assertive, challenging or direct approach with clients, or reshaping the supervisee's practice – for example, with more individual consultancy work, or with more organisation consulting, or publishing more within their field.

Individual and group supervision cannot be substituted for each other and cover quite different aspects of the supervisee's work. Relational reflections in terms of the supervisee–supervisor relationship, for example, come more strongly to the fore in individual supervision. An open discussion of this topic is a tall order with a group of onlookers. This reflection on the supervision relationship itself generally increases after the first few meetings. Parts of the supervision can then start to resemble coaching or counselling. In group supervision there is less risk of slipping into group therapy, because the case material remains centre-stage.

In my view, it is best to alternate individual and group supervision during a career in coaching and organisation consulting. It can be very productive to receive individual supervision for five years, say, and then to participate for a similar period in a supervision group, or in open supervision groups where you encounter different colleagues every time. I often see highly experienced colleagues organising their own groups, and hence a type of peer supervision or peer consultation, but I still wonder if that isn't a form of avoidance of responsibility: the responsibility to subject yourself regularly to really independent professional supervision.

Individual supervision can take place equally well over the telephone as face-to-face. The fact that we aren't looking at each other in a telephone conversation often means that we can associate more freely. In addition, both participants can take notes without distracting the conversation partner. In some ways telephone supervision is similar to therapy on the couch: it can feel more vulnerable and will generate deeper associations.

Group supervision by telephone is more difficult because much of the group is silent for extended periods – and you start to wonder in what way those silent participants are present. In addition, it raises the barrier for other group members wishing to interrupt the supervisee's account of his case.

In the remainder of this chapter I discuss three methods for organising supervision meetings:

- the *classical supervision method*: this method can be used for individual and group supervision;
- the *individual supervision method*: this method is simply a basic framework around and within an individual supervision session;
- the *group consultation method*: this method provides a structure for intensive supervision sessions in groups where members can also work together 'live' and hone their coaching skills in the process.

To the best of my knowledge, the classical supervision method has the longest tradition. It has been employed for several decades in psychoanalysis and the supervision of social workers (Kadushin 1976).[4] The classical supervision method is nowadays used mainly as a counselling or coach training approach, or is applied in a pared-down variation entailing less work for the supervisee – for example, just a verbal report or a tape-recording of a session with a client. It remains a very thorough form of supervision in my view, which appears to have additional power because the supervisee has to pay rigorous attention to the learning process. As a result, he develops new perspectives and

---

[4] See also Kutzik (1977a, 1977b) for an overview of the historical roots of supervision, going back to European medicine in the Enlightenment and US social work in the nineteenth century.

becomes aware of emotions and doubts at three separate times: while writing the report, while reading out the report and while discussing the report in supervision. And, optionally, a fourth time if he decides to produce a written summary of the outcome of the supervision meeting.

In the individual supervision method, it is very useful for supervisor and supervisee to prepare in advance. This is a prerequisite for classical supervision, at least for the supervisee, who, at the very least, is expected to bring a sheet of notes from a relevant consultancy or coaching session with him.

For my part, I think it should always be possible to send questions, accounts of sessions, contracts or reports in advance of individual supervision sessions. The supervisor can be expected to read this material sent in beforehand, and in my experience such preparatory work greatly enhances the outcome of an individual supervision session.

The peer consultation methods in my book *Learning with Colleagues* (de Haan 2004) can also be used in supervision. In this case the role of the peer consultation facilitator is assumed by the supervisor, who himself has to find appropriate times to bring up the familiar *ex cathedra* supervision observations (normative and restorative elements – see Chapter 1).

I notice myself, however, that I come back time and again to the group consultation method because it enables participants both to receive specific feedback on their coaching and to discuss a range of case material. The problem with peer consultation groups of consultants and coaches without an external (paid) facilitator is that no one is really concerned with putting a stop to any transgressions of ethical or personal boundaries – i.e. with the normative and restorative functions of supervisors.

An experienced peer consultation group without a facilitator is still a sanctuary for learning and exchanging best practice, but experience also shows that such groups ultimately become very 'friendly' and conflict-avoiding and therefore may fall short in confrontational feedback and discussion of the inevitable border disputes and transgressions.

Classical supervision method, individually or in groups

This method works for both individual and group supervision.

Table 6.1 Classical supervision method

Step	Description	Approximate time needed
1	**Introduction to the background of the case** The supervisor introduces the background of the assignment and client, usually describing the consultancy or coaching assignment in chronological order. This step may be superfluous if the supervision is individual and takes place frequently, e.g. every week.	15 mins
2	**Introduction to the recent case material** The supervisee reads out a written account of his consultancy or coaching session, prepared shortly after the session. An account is around two to four pages long and describes what was said in the session, and by whom, in their actual words as far as possible. The account is rendered anonymous to protect the client organisation. The supervisor and any group members can interrupt the supervisee with brief questions or summaries. They take notes while the supervisee reads the account.	20 mins
3	**Reflection on the case** The group reflects on the case material, under the supervisor's direction. The supervisor also acts as a facilitator for questions and answers between group members and the supervisee. The supervisor often accounts for the final part of this step by contributing his own observations and interpretations.	20 mins
4	**Review and evaluation** The group members review the supervision session: what was helpful? What worked well? What didn't work so well? If any sensitive information or emotional responses have arisen, the supervisor stays behind with the supervisee for a short while after the session. The supervisee can further enhance the benefits of the method by writing a summary of the supervision session later on.	5 mins
	Time needed (as a minimum):	60 mins

Individual supervision method

Table 6.2 Individual supervision method

Step	Description	Approximate time needed
1	**Establishing a contract and establishing rapport** Supervisee and supervisor check in with each other and enquire into how things are, what is relevant today, what else is going on. Sometimes they join forces to devise a structure for the session: which case material, which topics, etc. At this point (or sometimes by email prior to the session), more detailed written information on the materials can be submitted, such as accounts of sessions or psychometric data.	10 mins
2	**Discussion of recent case** The supervisee recounts a recent assignment. The supervisor joins in when he considers it time for a summary or if something occurs to him. If both think it is time to move on to the next case, the supervisee starts another account. Sometimes, due to pressure of time, a case is left unfinished and a final one is squeezed in with little time. This part of the session often feels a bit fraught, because there are so many perspectives, so much background which may be relevant, and the supervisor wants to share his own impressions with the supervisee as well.	60 mins
3	**Placing this session in the wider context** This step can also take place earlier or indeed be omitted. Supervisor and supervisee remind each other of the framework contract governing their sessions and the supervisee's long-term objectives.	20 mins
4	**Practical, housekeeping tasks** Including a brief evaluation of the session as a whole.	10 mins
	Time needed (as a minimum):	100 mins

Group consultation method

Table 6.3   Group consultation method

Step	Description	Approximate time needed
1	**Introduction of the issue and start of supervision** The supervisee introduces his issue with some brief context. One of the other group members offers to act as 'coach' to the contributor of the issue. Depending on the time available, they organize a 15- to 20-minute dialogue (step 2) in which the case can be explored.	5 mins
2	**Consultation** The coach explores the case by establishing a contract, summarizing, giving back observations and interpreting – more or less like an ordinary coaching session, but with an audience. The others, including the supervisor, take notes on the session and on issues they want to bring up later.	20 mins
3	**Reflection: feedback for the coach** The group reviews the coaching. After a brief opportunity for the two participants to 'blow off steam', the other group members review the consultation session and give the coach feedback. The supervisor notes what the participants say to the group while 'blowing off steam'; this often reveals aspects that the participants were preoccupied with but were not made explicit during step 2, as in the case example earlier in this chapter.	15 mins
4	**Reflection: further reflection for the supervisee** Under the supervisor's direction, the participants take another look at the case in question. What has the supervisee learned so far? Which aspects have been neglected? The supervisor uses this step to give normative and restorative supervision if necessary, in addition to the mainly formative supervision already given by the coach and the group (Proctor 1988).	15 mins
5	**Evaluation** This step comes only at the end of the meeting, after all the case material. The group reviews the process: experiences, effects of contributions from group members, etc. The supervisor can also ask for feedback.	5 mins
	Time needed (as a maximum per case):	60 mins

Summary

Step-by-step methods and detailed protocols are not helpful in supervision because supervision is much more about close observation and free association by the supervisee and supervisor, centred around the case material. In terms of method, therefore, the main ingredient is that there are always two or more slightly 'uneasy' people in the room who have no idea what is coming next.

Having said that, there are of course methodical aspects to the supervisor's work.

Group supervision:

- In group supervision, the session needs to be managed fairly tightly to get as many ideas as possible onto the table and to let the supervisor himself come into his own.
- The supervisor needs to find the right balance between facilitating a changing and evolving meeting of peers and other supervisory requirements, such as normative and restorative interventions.
- The supervisor regularly breaks through the convergent dynamic ('groupthink') in a group meeting.

Individual supervision:

- In individual supervision the supervisor needs to act as a facilitator in the background and give free rein to association.
- Individual supervision can take place equally well by telephone.

Group supervision is not a substitute for individual supervision, or vice versa. They are different paths to learning, on which we learn differently and learn different things.

In this chapter I discussed three commonly used supervision methods that have proved their worth in a wide range of contexts:

- The classical supervision method: this method is the most substantial that supervision has to offer. It is a reliable way of learning from your own case material.
- The individual supervision method: this method is more a framework around supervision sessions that leaves supervisor and supervisee as free as possible to pursue their important work.
- The group consultation method: this method is ideal for providing groups of consultants and coaches with supervision and allowing these colleagues to see each other in action and respond to each other's approaches as a coach/consultant during the meeting.

7 Ethical maturity and contracting for supervision: the full quality cycle

with Michael Carroll

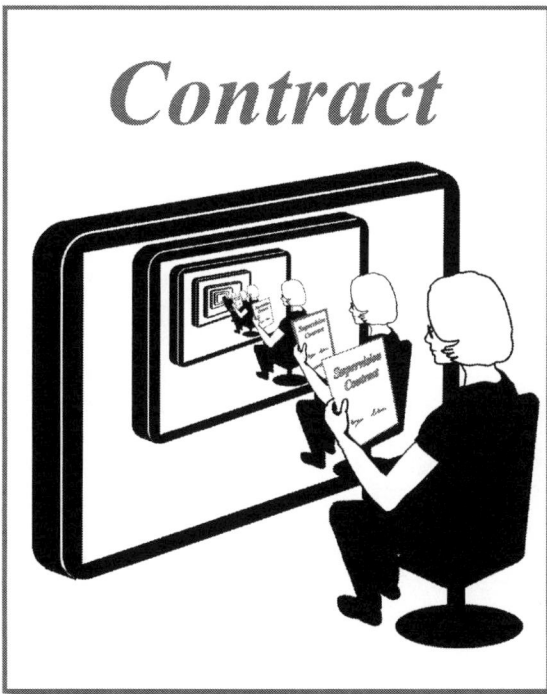

Contract

SUPERVISION AS...
Reflection on reflection on reflection

In this chapter we will review what ethical maturity means in the field of coaching and organisation supervision. In the second part of the chapter we will consider a number of formal instruments that support an ethical supervisory practice: contract, testimonial and review.

Ethical maturity

Supervision is an ethical experience, as is coaching, as is organisation development. As Aristotle suggested, ethics is part of our human quest, which is towards the good. Being responsible for what we do is part of being ethical and whatever diminishes or does away with responsibility in effect diminishes or does away with the ethical dimension of action. We see humans, individuals, groups, teams and organisations as responsible for their actions and therefore we call those actions good or bad, good or better – effectively ethical. Ethics demands consciousness – the ability to be aware of what is being done, having some insight into our intentions and being alert and watchful about when ethical issues, problems and dilemmas emerge.

In this chapter we will use the terms 'ethical' and 'moral' interchangeably in order to discuss cognitive and decision-making processes in terms of what is good and bad, right and wrong, or good and better in human behaviour as it takes place in individuals, groups and organisations. Engaging with the ethical field is like entering a minefield of uncertainty. From ancient times people have struggled with what ethics and morals mean and how ethical decisions are made. The moral and ethical questions we face today are similar to those which challenged our ancestors. Are there universal laws of good and bad that apply to us all? To all situations? What role does culture play in our ethical thinking? Are there stages of ethical development we go through as we progress through life? Do we move, like children, from ethical immaturity to ethical maturity? Are we born with ethical intelligence or do we learn what ethics means from our environments and upbringing? Will individuals in certain circumstances act morally differently than they would in different contexts? Are ethical decisions made consciously or unconsciously? Why are humans so destructive, cruel and even evil in their treatment of each other – where does unethical behaviour come from? Could we create the conditions and relationships that could result in individuals and groups acting unethically?

This chapter provides little scope to delve into most of these questions and space only allows us to focus on how supervisors can be ethically aware and make ethical decisions, given the complexity of the endeavour as outlined above. However, we want to keep the larger systemic picture in mind and work from the principle that there are many ethical theories and little agreement on what ethics means or how ethical decisions are made.

CASE EXAMPLE

Valerie supervises Jake. For some time she has been anxious about his work as an executive coach. On several occasions he has spoken in supervision about what, in her view, are rather serious boundary issues in his work with coachees. She has challenged him gently about these parameters:

- confidentiality where organisations are concerned and where he often shared information with human resource directors or managers without clear permission from his coachee;
- relationship boundaries where he will unthinkingly have lunch or dinner with coachees;
- location issues where he will meet clients in hotel lobbies; and
- a situation, now over, where he had a sexual relationship with a former coachee (not during the coaching relationship time).

Jake has dismissed her concerns, justifying his actions by saying that the kinds of contexts in which he works and the particular client group he sees demand high levels of flexibility on his part. He is not being unethical, he maintains, but adaptable. And as for the sexual relationship, that took place after the coaching relationship had finished and therefore was not unethical according to the codes he has read. Valerie wonders what she should do. She decides to work with Jake from a less confrontational but more educational perspective and asks him to do two things: scenario-play some possibilities where boundaries are breached to the detriment of the coaching relationship and look in more detail at where Jake's freedom to be the coach he wants to be is compromised. Jake quite enjoys the challenge and as he plays out different scenarios and possibilities (like imagining himself in front of a jury justifying why he did what he did), a number of insights hit him. He begins to realise that he has been 'mixing up' various types of relationship: personal, social and professional lines have been blurred. This has resulted in behaviours that have confused others about what kind of relationship they have and what roles and responsibilities come with that particular relationship. He also realises that professionally he has been compromising his credibility and influence with clients by keeping contracts vague and unclear. Also, he has not been strong at providing good emotional containment where clients feel safe. In particular, he has found it difficult to resolve ethical dilemmas where there has been a clash of values – for example, the need for confidentiality versus his requirement to give feedback to the company. Over time Valerie notices how the quality of Jake's ethical stance grows considerably and how he pauses before making decisions, to spend time reflecting on them, where before he was quite impulsive in the decisions he made. He is becoming good at reviewing the ethical decisions he has made and using them as springboards for ongoing learning.

For many people, and Jake initially was one, ethics is about conformity to ethical codes. If the code says it is forbidden then it is forbidden; if the code doesn't forbid it then it is acceptable. Most professionals belong to professional bodies that provide ethical codes for their members. These codes and frameworks usually contain principles to guide members in making ethical decisions as well as clear, unambiguous directives on what should or should not be done in certain circumstances. However, being a paid-up member of a profession and subscribing to its code of ethics does not guarantee ethical behaviour. It is part of the human condition sometimes to know what we should do without actually doing it. We also, at times, know what we shouldn't do and still do it. And there are times when we are morally confused and just don't know what to do. Even when we behave ethically, we are sometimes unable to articulate why we did what we did or explain coherently the processes that went into our decision-making that resulted in action. We cannot always justify, defend or explain our actions. And finally, even when we can explain what we did and connect it to the guidelines and principles, we can be unsure that we did the right thing – we are not always at peace with the moral decision(s) we make. Hindsight, after-action reviews and occasional rumination keep our previous ethical decisions alive for us and we can easily end up replaying them obsessively. On the positive side, we can use recall to enable retrospective insight in order to learn from ethical decisions already made.

Five procedures are outlined above, all of which are needed if we are to look beyond decision-making in ethics to what we are calling ethical maturity. They are:

1   Fostering ethical sensitivity and watchfulness: creating ethical antennae that keep us alert to when ethical issues or dilemmas are present.

2   Being able to make an ethical decision in line with our ethical principles and our values.

3   Implementing the ethical decision(s) made.

4   Being able to articulate and justify to stakeholders the reasons why the ethical decisions were made and implemented.

5   Achieving closure on the event and being at peace with it even when there were other possible decisions or better decisions that could have been made. Learning from what has happened and living with the consequences of decisions made.

These five components make up, in our view, what we are calling *ethical maturity*. We define ethical maturity as having the reflective, rational, emotional and intuitive capacity to decide whether actions are right and wrong, or good and better, having the resilience and courage to implement those decisions, being accountable for ethical decisions made (publicly or privately) and being able to learn from and live with the experience(s).

This is not a sequential model in that we move from component 1 (being ethically watchful) through to component 5 (being at peace with the ethical decision made) and then beginning the process all over again when faced with the next moral issue. The components intertwine and interweave. These are not stages or steps in a chronological sequence but ethical elements that influence one another. However, there is some chronology involved: implementing a decision clearly comes after a decision has been made and, in turn, coming to terms with the decision comes after making and implementing the decision. Other than that, there is interconnection and influence throughout. We become morally sensitive by making decisions, our peaceful acceptance of our past behaviours itself influences our moral stances. Figure 7.1 outlines the components and shows some of their connections.

The above definition of ethical maturity needs a bit of unpacking. The first four features of the person making mature ethical decisions are an ability to reflect, to use reason, to be in touch with emotions and to monitor our intuitive or tacit decision-making processes. Reflection is a specific human endeavour that allows us to stand back and observe and generate meaning from a distance. It involves a mindful stance that activates our curiosity and inquisitiveness. It is our human way of making sense of experience (see Chapter 3 and Carroll 2009, 2010). Zero reflection is a slippery slope to possible unethical stances – we fall into habitual and mindless ways of behaving that are not thought through or reflected upon in order to consider other meanings and other possible actions. Reflection brings mindfulness, attention and deliberation to the process of ethical decision-making. In supervision, Valerie encourages Jake to step back from his involvement in one of his executive coaching arrangements and begin to reflect from various positions: to see things from the coachee's perspective, from the viewpoint of the organisation and so on. She helps him to think systemically, get inside the values of his professional body, and consider it legally. Jake learns over time that reflection-on-action is his way of deriving multiple meanings from the same event so that he can have as much information as possible before making his decisions.

Using our rational, reasonable and logical faculties is a further feature or characteristic of ethical maturity. This includes the ability to work logically and thoughtfully

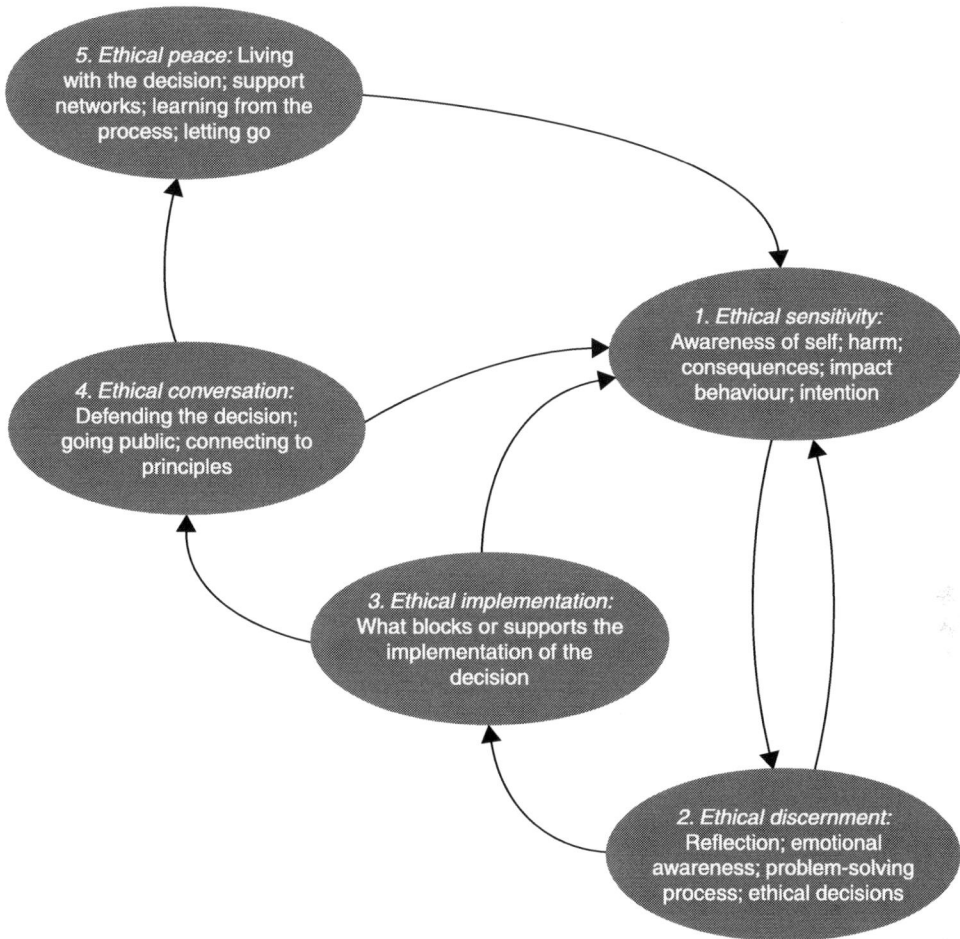

Figure 7.1 An overview of the five components in ethical maturity suggested in this chapter, and of how they might interact during ethical decision making and practice.

towards conclusions and decisions. Thinking critically, examining in detail using rational approaches, is a key feature of being human and one of our best gifts. It is this feature that makes us different from other animals who act according to rigid codes of conduct built into their lives. Rationality is our ability to reason, to reflect, to imagine and to consider in depth why we should choose one course of action over another. Valerie asks Jake incisive questions that make him think through his decisions, logically and rationally. She asks him at times to imagine he is in front of a judge who is demanding solid explanations for why he did what he did. This forces Jake to think rationally and give reasoned arguments for his decisions.

However, while important, rational deliberation is not the only faculty we need to arrive at ethical maturity. In fact, rational reflection may lead us away from sound principles by building up an illusionary and self-serving argument. To be in touch with our emotions and those of others in terms of what is happening is a further dimension we consider crucial to ethical decision-making. While the history of ethical and moral understanding often gives little sway to emotions in making ethical decisions, our awareness of the role of emotions in decision-making in general has increased over the years and insights from neuroscience have helped us place emotion more centrally in the making of ethical decisions – for example, 'The madman (as Chesterton remarked) is not the man who has lost his reason. The madman is the man who has lost everything except his reason. After the emotions have made their decision the rational circuits in the cortex are activated. People come up with persuasive reasons to justify their moral intuition' (Lehrer 2009: 165). Connected to emotion are our intuitive senses where decisions are made unconsciously or using the adaptive unconscious (Wilson 2002). These are fast and instinctual decisions that come from who we are and from our moral characters. Valerie continually asks Jake to stay with his feeling and emotions and see what information comes from them. In fact, she has helped him monitor his immediate reactions to events in his coaching and OD work and he has found that his first emotions are often accurate reactions to what is happening.

Intuition also plays a large part in ethical decision-making. In fact there are convincing indications that many (if not most) decisions are made intuitively before our conscious mind notes, validates and justifies them using reason and language (Wilson 2002; Lehrer 2009). Learning to trust our intuitive responses – those responses built on past experience, current observations and mindfulness, as well as staying in touch with our feelings – becomes an important element in ongoing professional development. Some (e.g. Schön 1983; Atkinson and Claxton 2000) have suggested that more experienced practitioners make decisions intuitively while beginners and novices have to 'think through' what they do. In supervision, Valerie asks Jake to monitor, stay with and articulate his intuitive responses. He finds out quickly that he usually has an intuitive response that he can trust. Recently, he trusted an immediate hunch that one of his executive coachees was unwell and suggested he see his doctor, who discovered that his headaches stemmed from a growing tumour on his brain (his manager's and Jake's initial response before seeing the client was that his headaches were due to overwork and a very demanding travel schedule).

In making ethical decisions it is worth noting the difference between intention and action. Fine (2007: 64) captures this beautifully in her work on the brain: 'Our appraisals of others also fail to take the same generous account of good intentions that we allow ourselves . . . they [volunteers in a research project] generously judged themselves by what they wanted to do, rather than by what they actually did . . . we give others less credit for their good intentions than we give ourselves for ours. The masterful hypocrisy of the immoral brain demands a certain grudging respect. It lazily applies nothing but the most superficial and disapproving analysis of others' misdemeanours, while bending over backwards to reassure that you can do no wrong'. Valerie, again, keeps Jake looking at the actions and events of his work, as well as his intentions. He has noticed at times how these two – what he intends to do and what he actually does – can be out of alignment. A recent example was when he challenged an executive he was working with who told him he was harassing rather than helpful. This put Jake in touch with his tendency to overdo confrontation, especially when his client was not moving at his (Jake's) pace.

Focusing on one of these four – reason, emotion, reflection and intuition – to the detriment of the others can result in missing key ethical points. Concentrating on reason alone can end up out of the relationship and unreflective. Concentrating on emotion alone can result in being driven by impulsivity. Concentrating on reflection alone can lead to navel-gazing and introspection that stays inward-looking. Concentrating on intuition alone can terminate in behaviours that are not thought through rationally and logically.

Supervisors help supervisees make sense of and understand the five components of ethical maturity outlined above. In doing so, they and their supervisees are committing themselves to high standards and excellent practice by building moral character – which is not always attained by simply keeping to ethical codes which too often ask for the lowest common denominator (fall below this standard and you are acting unethically). How can supervisors support themselves and their supervisees in being competent in each of the components? The following are some guidelines for each component.

Component 1: fostering ethical sensitivity

Building a moral compass and fostering ethical sensitivity entails:

- Awareness of my own current values (religious, role models, from family, work, home). This is not just awareness of espoused values, the values I say I believe in, but my values-in-action, the real values to which I subscribe.[1]
- Awareness of why I do what I do – our motivation. Why do I do what I do? What motivates me to do it? Knowing my own hidden agendas can help me notice when I am tempted to be less than ethically mature (e.g. I love the power this gives me, how flattered I can be that I am needed, etc.).
- Knowing how I tend to use power (power over, power with) can give insights into when I might feel the need to rescue or give answers or be authoritative when needed.
- Taking care of myself, physically, emotionally, mentally and spiritually, means I have the energy I need to think and feel clearly and puts me in a stronger place to notice ethical problems and dilemmas when they arise.
- Embracing my own fear and my hypocrisies allows me to recognise and accept some of my limitations.
- Being able to reflect deeply and honestly can support me when my own needs predominate.
- Having sufficient empathy to keep me ethically sensitive and allow me to see from other perspectives. Compassion also builds moral sensitivity.

---

[1] In *Existentialism and Human Emotions* (1957) Sartre writes, 'To choose this or that is to affirm at the same time the value of what we choose, because we can never choose evil'.

- Staying 'in relationship with' others, rather than just relating to them, means I see them as individuals with differences rather than as objects or commodities.

Component 2: discerning ethical decisions

The ability to make mature ethical decisions requires:

- Being open: standing back and keeping bigger pictures in view (thinking individually, relationally and systemically), helps me to make better decisions.
- Using others to help me make clear decisions, via supervision, consultancy, codes, etc.
- Slowing down the pace, reflecting and keeping tabs on what is happening to me and others.
- An awareness of how I tend to make decisions in general. This can help me understand my strengths and my limitations in decision-making, when to harness the former and when to acknowledge the latter.
- Accessing my feelings, hunches and intuitions to see if there is a clear and definitive answer without going to deliberation and conscious decision-making.
- Noticing external pressures on me to make a decision one way or another: this may help me pause and rethink a decision.
- Trusting my intuition.

Component 3: implementing ethical decisions

Implementing ethical decisions means being alert to:

- The possible gap between deciding what to do and actually implementing the decision.
- What might stop or block the building of a bridge between decision and action.
- What stops and blocks me in this instance (e.g. fear, lack of time, collusion, competing values, fear of repercussions, ambiguity).
- Procrastination about the implementation of decisions and what that might tell me.
- The competing commitment that stops me moving forward with my decision. What fears do I need to face that might prevent me acting?

Component 4: justifying and defending the decision I made

Accountability for decisions made is enhanced by:

- Keeping a journal and/or reflective notes to maintain tabs on what is happening.
- Not becoming defensive but being honest and noticing where there are risks, lack of clarity and differences in viewpoints.
- Allowing conflict and disagreement and holding my own.

- Imaging myself: providing rationales for decisions made, which helps to clarify why I did what I did.
- Anything that helps me to move from a defensive position to one of openness, curiosity and honesty. This step could demand great courage if I felt that I had not made the right decision or factors had influenced me in making a decision that was not the best one.

Component 5: ethical peace and sustainability

Living with decisions made means:

- Living with lingering doubts and uncertainty while still being able to rehearse other scenarios and other possible endings and decisions.
- Continuing to learn from what happened even if it means reopening the case and reviewing it in the light of new experiences or new information.
- Being self-accepting and understanding that I am dealing with issues that often have no right answers.
- Avoiding rumination and obsessive reflection through strategies such as meditation, taking exercise, enjoying nature, pets or hobbies.
- Accepting that I am limited: I tolerate uncertainty, ambiguity and the contexts in which things happen.
- Being compassionate towards myself.
- Using writing and journal-keeping to articulate my thoughts and feelings.
- Having places where I can speak about the issues and get the support I need to deal with whatever decisions are made.
- Using mistakes, poor decisions I have already made and hindsight to learn how to let go of perfectionism.
- Recognising if any apologies are needed.
- Accepting that I would make a different decision now, were I to make the decision again.
- Being able to let go and forgive.

Here is another example from our practice that may help to sharpen your 'ethical maturity'. What would you do if you were the supervisor?

CASE EXAMPLE

Jim worked with Alex, an executive coach, four years ago in a coaching relationship paid for by his (Jim's) company which lasted six months. From all perspectives the coaching, focused as it was on Jim's leadership qualities, went well. It was clear at that stage that he was having some problems with his immediate boss, even though this was never a direct focus in coaching. Now, more than four years on, Alex has been asked by the company lawyers to provide his notes on the coaching sessions. Jim is in the process of a grievance procedure against the employer. Alex is unsure about his legal and ethical responsibilities regarding the request just made. He still has his session notes and post-session logbook from that time and he regrets that he has written some comments he would now not like anyone else to read (e.g. 'he looked depressed today' and 'I understand why some see him as a difficult character to get on with' and 'abrasive in his management style'). He brings the issue to supervision, his main worry being that he could be called as a witness for the company.

One thing Alex did take from the discussion at supervision was a new realisation about note-taking: from now on he intends to write all his notes in such a manner that clients, sponsors and others could read them without doubting his professionalism – i.e. he wants to be more specific and less opinionated in his notes.

Contracting and reviewing supervision

An important aspect of ethical practice is for the supervisor to manage the boundaries of the supervisory work professionally, with some important tools at his disposition: contracts, testimonials and (formal) reviews. Reaching agreement on the contract, and monitoring it, is even more important in supervision than in consultancy and coaching. This is due in particular to the normative gatekeeper function of the supervisor (see Chapter 1). It is advisable always to use clear forms and careful data recording, including session notes and logbooks. Supervisors are also well advised, as in organisation consultancy and coaching, to make sure that such information is carefully stored and protected, because it may be requested by clients and third parties (with the client's consent), and that it is destroyed or rendered unreadable after a set time has elapsed.

Precisely because the role of supervisor is so multi-layered, it is important to conclude a contract that is as clear as possible, and to review it regularly. A contract needn't be long (see, for example, our contracting checklist on p. 115).[2] If one embarks on supervision without such a contract there is always a risk that completely different ideas about the purpose of the sessions remain implicit and start affecting the supervisory relationship. Contracts ensure that all involved in supervision are 'singing from the same hymn sheet'. For instance, one of us (Erik) recalls his own frustration 'When one of my supervisors made our sessions highly educational and abstract, while I'd have preferred to talk about and learn from my recent practice material'. (For an example of a supervision contract see Carroll and Gilbert 2005: Appendix A.)

A contract is also important as 'evidence': every supervision contract can be used as a bridge to other interested parties, who may not participate in the supervision directly but nevertheless have something to gain from it, such as the supervisee's clients,

---

[2] See Sills (2011) and Skinner (2011) for a fuller introduction to contracting in coaching, including administrative, developmental and sessional contracts and multi-party contracting.

colleagues and managers, and the wider organisational and social context of the supervisee consultancy work. It is therefore good practice to draw up a supervision contract in response to the first session and, after sending it to the supervisee, to make a point of asking if it needs any fine-tuning. Contracts are only sent to others in the organisation after the supervisee has given his explicit consent.[3]

Just as with ethical codes and codes of conduct, we need to understand in the first instance that it is not possible to cover every eventuality with a paper document. Indeed, rules on paper are no guarantee of an honest, sound and well-coordinated practice. However good the underlying contracts, supervision relationships are determined mainly by the 'psychological contract' (Rousseau 1995) maintained by the supervisor and supervisee (independently!). The psychological contract can be defined as 'everything we have not put down on paper' – i.e. as a collection of unwritten expectations between parties working together. A psychological contract is not only much broader than a paper contract but, in general, it is also more relevant to the supervision relationship and its outcome. The degree of trust that a supervisee has in his supervisor is of vital importance, but can't be laid down in a contract. Nor can a basic appreciation of the supervisor, or a degree of tolerance if the supervisor is barking up the wrong tree, or has failed to grasp the case history, or understand the client. We can certainly write down the words, but that wouldn't make any difference to the way in which emotions and trust continue to evolve within the relationship (for more on the psychological contract in supervision see also Carroll and Gilbert 2005).

In our view, there is always a certain tension between explicit and implicit agreement – i.e. between the written contract and the psychological contract; a tension that may lead to problems in supervisory or consulting relationships and trigger diminishing effectiveness.[4] As soon as your implicit expectations as a supervisee are no longer fulfilled, you become less open in sharing your client experience and less receptive to new perspectives on your practice.

For this reason alone, it is useful to set out arrangements and expectations in a contract and to review the contract in written form at a later stage (e.g. when drawing up the *supervisor's testimonial* or at final review). The initial contract will provide a further opportunity for careful reflection, in the knowledge that the outcome of that reflection may be shared with others and may even have to be approved by them. But the main reasons for concluding contracts are the potentially far-reaching consequences of the work for the supervisee's clients, such as failure to achieve promotion, dismissal procedures, workplace conflicts or suspicion of fraud. In all of these cases, it can never be ruled out that the role of the coach or consultant and consequently the supervision of this coach or consultant by the supervisor may be examined by mandated authorities.

---

[3] The way in which our contracting checklist focuses attention individually on the supervisee's successes, his clients and his clients' organisations, is derived from a principle proposed by Peter Hawkins.

[4] See the examples of counterproductive events in supervision in Gray *et al.* (2001). Time after time, it appears that at moments like these the supervisee hopes for more empathy and listening ability and experiences a degree of rejection from his supervisor.

Contracts, reviews and testimonials are essential in the supervision relationship, even though they are not its principal ingredient. From a relational perspective, a written contract functions as a boundary on the sessions, just like the time limitation and the asymmetry in the supervisory relationship. A boundary means a restriction, of course, but also containment (Bion 1963). The contract therefore provides not only a framework but also nourishment and protection for what is contained within the limits of the contract. The supervision contract is thus one of the many basic preconditions (such as time, space, confidentiality, asymmetry and methodology) that help to maintain focus and concentration on the client material. For example, the contract helps by capturing in words the themes and development that the supervisee envisages in the longer term. As with any boundary, there is a dual purpose: maintaining the attention devoted to those underlying themes and arousing special attention when the sessions stray beyond the agreed objectives.

Just like reflections in supervision relationships, contracts in supervision inevitably start to refer to themselves. When the two participants talk about their contract, they are effectively engaging in 'meta-contracting'. This happens again later when the participants evaluate the contract or draw up testimonials. Moreover, they are implicitly rewriting the supervision contract in the process. Just as in parallel processes in relationships, we often see the development of a recursive process in which new perspectives are generated by meta-reflections.

In comparison with the formal contracting checklist (see Figure 7.2), one of us (Erik) writes his contract more in the style of a personal letter, but the points covered are the same as those in the form.

Formal contracting is a one-off event and can be seen as separate from the actual supervision. The other two documents in this chapter, however, are much more an integral part of supervision and can be regarded as an extension or conclusion of the supervision work in paper form.

- The *supervisor's testimonial* (see Figure 7.3) requires the supervisor to reflect on his own observations over many sessions, sum up those observations and reflections and commit them to paper. This reflection-on-reflection should ideally follow seamlessly from the work done by the supervisor during the sessions.
- In the same way, the *supervision review form* (see Figure 7.4) requires the supervisee to consider his own reflections and what he has learned over a prolonged period of supervision, and to set it down in a written report.

Completing both the supervisor's testimonial and the review form is still very much part of supervision: nothing more or less than a continuation of the sessions by other means. The supervision review form challenges the supervisee to generate new reflections in response to the joint reflection process, while the supervisor's testimonial obliges the supervisor to express his own reflections in writing. As a rule, both supervisor and supervisee find completing their respective forms a challenging process. They do have to overcome a barrier, because the reflections in these two documents take on a more formal character, become set in stone by being written down, evolve less freely than verbal reflections, and (may) start to lead a life of their own as a permanent witness to

Contracting checklist

Name of supervisee: ....

Name of supervisor: ....

Main purpose of supervision: ....
....

The supervision will be successful for the supervisee if: ....
....

The supervision will be successful for the supervisee's clients if: ....
....

The supervision will be successful for the supervisee's clients' organisations if:...................
....

Role and contribution of the supervisor: ....
....

Structure, place, frequency and length of sessions: ....
....

Confidentiality agreement: ....
....

Review process for outcomes: ....
....

Testimonials and data protection: ....
....

Number of sessions and fee structure:...

Date and signature: ....

Figure 7.2 Model contracting checklist

Supervisor's testimonial

Name of supervisee: ....

Name of supervisor: ....

Valid for period: ....

Dates of supervision sessions: ....

....

Average length of sessions: ....

....

Description of supervisor's role: ....

....

....

....

Strengths of supervisee as a consultant/coach: ....

....

....

With a special commendation for: ....

....

....

Areas for development in the forthcoming year:...

....

....

....

Date and signature: ....

Figure 7.3 Model supervisor's testimonial

Supervision review form

1   What difference has supervision made to date in your practice? What are you most proud of? What have you started to do more, or differently?

....

....

2   What effect has this had on those around you (e.g. your clients, colleagues, boss or family)?

....

....

3   If you look at the expectations you had beforehand, a year ago or when we started supervision, how well has supervision met your expectations?

Mark an 'X' on the following scale from 1 to 10:

1   10
Not met   Far exceeded
expectations   expectations

4   Could you highlight and briefly describe one critical moment in your supervisory journey: a moment that was tense, exciting, a breakthrough or a rupture, or significant to you in any other way?

....

....

What made this moment critical for you? ....

....

What was the context in which this critical moment emerged? ....

....

How did we handle the critical incident?...

....

What was the eventual outcome? ....

....

5   What was it about the way you and your supervisor worked together that you found most helpful?

....

....

For our research into coaching and supervision interventions, we would like to make use of your responses to these questions, without ever mentioning anything specific about yourself, your organisation or the supervisory relationship. If you object to our use of these data in this general and anonymous way, please let us know by ticking this box:

❏ I object to the use of these data for research purposes.

Thank you!

Figure 7.4   Supervision review form

the supervisory relationship. It is advisable to handle such reflections in black and white with caution and not to pressurise the supervisee unnecessarily into producing such material. The fear of stifling or paralysing reflections is justified and understandable.

The example of the supervisor's testimonial given on page 116 is worded as positively as possible. In addition, we make sure that our supervisee is aware in advance of any criticisms or areas where we believe more work is needed, because they have already been raised in the sessions. The supervisee is always the first to see the testimonial. Only once he is entirely happy with it, or if we have no other option due to a difference of opinion with our supervisee, are other parties such as the supervisee's clients or manager given access to the testimonial. In the end it is our personal testimony, but in the vast majority of cases supervisee and supervisor are in complete agreement on the content. If there is disagreement concerning the testimonial, such disagreement can safely be assumed to extend to the supervisee's practice, and usually to the supervision relationship itself. As we see confirmed time after time, all of our working relationships are closely intertwined through parallel processes (see Chapter 2).

In the model supervision review form (see p. 117), almost all of the questions are open. These questions aim to get the supervisee, and then the supervisor himself, thinking about how to describe the outcome of the supervision. One question focuses on a brief description of a single 'moment' of supervision that was critical or crucial in some way. In the same way that, in supervision, one relationship often stands for a multitude of other relationships, or a single unalterable Relationship (with a capital 'R') from the past: a single moment often stands for the essence of the supervision assignment as a whole.

CASE EXAMPLE

For a number of years, this international humanitarian organisation has implemented a leadership development programme that places a strong emphasis on personal growth and OD – in other words, on a balance between task and team, or between what role and relationships require of the leader. All senior leaders taking part in the programme are assigned a personal coach who draws up a short formal contract, engages in a number of coaching conversations and interviews a number of direct colleagues, while encouraging the client to do the same, with a view to gaining a team perspective on the managers.

The coaches working on the programme receive 'shadow consulting' from a supervisor who was a coach on the programme in the past. As the coaches work in different countries these supervisory conversations are all scheduled as two-hour teleconferences.

There are some 25 coaches on the project and they each work with five or more leaders. They are supervised in groups of three to five. Supervision sessions by and large follow the same structure. After a brief 'check in' the supervisor explores the requests for supervision and then asks the coaches to work together in pairs, according to the group supervision method (see Chapter 6, p. 101) or if there are many requests, to engage in a freer enquiry within the full group. During the final 20 minutes the group decides when to meet next and the supervisor collects 'themes from group supervision' for the steering group of the change process, with the help of four questions:

1   How are the participants engaging with the process?
2   What seems to be figural for participants at this time?
3   What organisational themes are emerging or illuminated by the process?
4   Are there any challenges that coaches are experiencing where the steering group might help?

In this way, themes that can be identified by several coaches in the group are collected. While during the previous part of the session there is an agreement of strict confidentiality, at data collection non-attributable themes are collected for sharing with others in the organisation, starting with the steering group. Shortly after every session the supervisor creates a draft document, which is signed off or amended by the coaches. Only when they are all happy with the summary is the document relayed to the steering committee overlooking the change process. In this way the steering group can identify some important themes that are emerging for leaders and coaches, without being able to trace them back to individuals. Moreover, this process helps the coaches themselves keep track of what is going on in the wider process, to keep the finger on the pulse and learn from each other which aspects of the programme may be relevant or challenging for their clients. At the moment, themes that are identified are mainly to do with the large number of change initiatives, the pressure on change coming from the top of the organisation and the bureaucracy that is somehow stalling or working against change, even if this appears against the wishes of all involved. As supervisory relationships deepen and sessions follow on each other, the supervisor is himself increasingly asked about what other groups have found. He feels free to answer those questions as he, like everyone else, can rely on a rich collection of relevant, anonymous, non-attributable findings.

Supervision is a forum for quality assurance, a place where supervisees are accountable for the work they do and the quality of that work. Making mature ethical and moral decisions about coaching and OD practice is undoubtedly part and parcel of that stance and adds value to the professional and the profession, not to mention the individual and organisational clients. For us, ethical maturity is not just about good-enough practice, but also about attaining excellent standards without being perfectionist. Contracting in supervision is an essential area of ethical practice that ensures clarity of roles and relationships and provides a 'safe emotional container' where supervisors and supervisees work together in agreed ways. Contracts also build in accountability elements (using testimonials and evaluations) so that supervision is not only about excellent practice but is seen to be so as well.

Summary

Ethical practice in supervision, or practising with *ethical maturity*, entails five competencies.

1   Fostering ethical sensitivity and watchfulness.
2   Making an ethical decision aligned to our ethical principles and our values.
3   Implementing the ethical decision(s) made.
4   Articulating and justifying to stakeholders the reasons why the ethical decisions were made and implemented.
5   Achieving closure on the event and being at peace with it even when there were other, possibly better, decisions that could have been made.

The following three documents can support the ethically mature practice of a supervisor:

- The supervision contract:
  - marks the start of the supervision relationship;
  - important because the relationship involves an element of assessment (the supervisor's function as a gatekeeper);
  - important as a 'bridge' to other interested parties;
  - important as a way of making boundaries on the supervisory relationship explicit: the contract provides concentration, focus and *containment*;
  - important as there is so much it does not cover: the *psychological contract*.
- The supervisor's testimonial and the supervision review form by the supervisee:
  - mark the passing of time within supervision and/or the end of the relationship;
  - are a written continuation of supervision;
  - oblige supervisor and supervisee to review their own reflections thoroughly and to engage in meta-reflection;
  - provide a helpful contrast with the more fluid, evolving form of supervision sessions but can therefore take on a life of their own.

In this chapter we have given examples of the kind of checklists that we use in our practice:

1   The contracting checklist gives a short list of items to include in a contract.
2   The supervisor's testimonial gives structure to the supervisor's testimony concerning the supervisee and the latter's practice.
3   The supervision review form provides a guideline for evaluation by the supervisee.

Appendix A: The history of transference and parallel process

As shown in Chapters 2 and 4 and various other places in this book, transference – the phenomenon whereby other relationships outside the room are reflected or copied, unconsciously, in this relationship, within the room – is encouraged in a special way by supervision. Supervision is characterised by reflection within a 'helping' relationship on other 'helping' relationships. By definition, transference may play a role in such reflection. For this reason, I believe every supervisor should take time to explore and understand the phenomenon of transference. As a supervisor it can give you a clearer picture of what is happening in your relationship with supervisees, but also between supervisees and the people they work with. Understanding transference also allows you to minimise certain risks that are described in the adjacent field of executive coaching but are nonetheless very real for supervisors, such as misjudgement of transference, overestimation of own abilities or abuse of power by the helping professional (Berglas 2002).

A quantitative empirical study by Doehrman (1976) found transference in the form of parallel processes in each of the supervisory relationships studied, and concludes as follows:

> For Mr Farley [a therapist] the parallel process phenomenon was exhibited not only in what his patient stirred up in him, which he then acted out with his supervisor, nor only in what his supervisor stirred in him, which he then carried into his relationship with his patient, but also in his relationship with his personal therapist, in his relationship to his other supervisor, and even in his relationship to the research interviewer. All these factors converged in the interactions between Mr Farley and his patient. If there is any one conclusion all these findings add up to, it is that the parallel process phenomenon occurs and recurs in a remarkable multiplicity of forms. At the very least, one comes away from this material with a sense of humility about the complexity, subtlety, and depth of human relationships. One is struck by the multifaceted nature of what on the surface seems to be a simple and even rather limited human relationship. Having discovered this order of complexity in a seemingly limited human relationship, one wonders about the complexities that must infuse other human affairs.

(p. 104)

To learn about transference, it is useful to go right back to the source of the concept and study the earliest writings about this phenomenon, in particular Freud's technical papers. The story of the discovery of transference is very instructive in itself, because it describes a number of unavoidable patterns that crop up again and again in the development of every supervisor and during every relationship entered into by supervisor and supervisee. We start with an overview of the discoveries made concerning transference: from the very first mention of the term in 1905 to half a century or so later, in 1955 and 1965, when the related terms 'parallel process' and 'working alliance' were introduced. Based on the history of these discoveries, we then look at what today's supervisor can do, when entering into a new supervisory relationship, with the insights gained from transference phenomena. The purpose of this appendix is therefore to improve our understanding of transference, but also to learn from Freud's discoveries and the knowledge subsequently acquired in this field.

Over the past few decades, impressive empirical evidence has been gathered which objectively demonstrates the phenomenon of transference. For an overview of these convincing results, see Andersen and Berk (1998) and Kraus and Chen (2010).

Freud, the discoverer of transference

Zur Dynamik der Übertragung (Freud 1912) is without doubt Freud's core text in the area of transference. In it, he defines transference as that part (or those parts) of the person's highly individual,[1] highly personal and largely unconscious loving impulses that is not being satisfied in existing relationships. According to Freud, transference is extremely individual for a number of reasons: the modelling after previous relationships, the unconscious underlying motivation and the link with thwarted libido. He assures us there is nothing special about the phenomenon, except for two 'problems'. First, neurotic people have more thwarted loving impulses, and therefore more intensive transference. Second, transference becomes the strongest resistance against treatment in psychoanalysis – even though it is originally an important bearer of healing and a condition for success. According to Freud (1912), the client is first to become aware of precisely that part of his resistance that translates into transference. The example that Freud gives more than once is the faltering of free association, which can point to thoughts about the therapist. Time and time again, he points out, when pathogenic material is approached, that part of the pathology that can be translated into transference will be the first to manifest itself consciously and will be defended most vigorously. In other words, the neurosis tries to defend itself by wrapping itself up in transference, by 'becoming' transference – i.e. the relationship offered to the therapist becomes the neurosis. The consequence is that conflicts with the neurosis will have to be fought out (in other words, healing needs to be done) in transference, within this very relationship, here and now. Victory in that conflict, Freud assures us, heralds an enduring cure of the neurosis.[2]

---

[1] He writes literally that everyone will repeat one or more of such 'clichés' regularly in the course of a lifetime (Freud 1912).

[2] In *Zur Einleitung der Behandlung* (1913) Freud examines this more closely and argues that if and only if the full intensity of transference is used to overcome resistance, it becomes impossible for the patient to persist in the neurosis, even after the transference has been resolved – i.e. after the treatment.

For Freud (1917), transference is always the same thing (*'immer das Gleiche'*) which will never 'allow its origins to be mistaken': it is libido streaming back from the symptoms – through heightened understanding of them – and into the relationship with the therapist.

Freud (1912) essentially distinguishes two types of transference: positive, loving[3] transference and negative, hostile transference. The loving variety comprises two further varieties, one associated with *eros* (erotic transference; see also Freud 1915), and one with *agape* (friendly transference). Transference is always there, from the very start of the cure. In the initial phases, loving transference represents the 'strongest drive to the work' (Freud 1917) – later on, it may become an obstacle as it attracts additional libido from freed symptoms, defences and resistances. Negative transference occurs in only a minority of cases, and usually somewhat later in the cure.

The history of the discoveries related to transference and counter-transference seems to be transferential in itself, as it is clearly a repetition of the same process of overcoming or eliminating obstacles (Freud, 1917):

1   First obstacle (before 1890): the problem is (related to) something in the unconscious, a hidden feeling or wish. Pills don't work, hypnosis doesn't last, arguing with the patient – even if successful – only instils an idea *next* to the unconscious, and doesn't really touch it. Solution: (1) try to map that unconscious by listening closely and with dedication; (2) uncover some of the suppressed material; and (3) make it more conscious. Then you can work with it more directly.

2   Second obstacle (after 1890): the flow of information dries up, memory does not give in or give away its treasures. At such a moment one discovers *defences* – e.g. when a memory is repressed. Solution: bring the defensive behaviour into the session and explore it with the client.

3   Third obstacle (around 1895): remembering halts again as it touches on something painful, embarrassing or contrary to morality, and the patient becomes hesitant. This points to *resistance*. Solution: overcome this resistance by guessing or intuiting it,[4] and naming it. Historically, this discovery coincided with the start of the 'fundamental rule' of free association (Freud's earlier technique was found to invite unnecessary resistance by its directive nature).

4   Fourth obstacle (after 1900): the flow of information halts again, or becomes repetitive. A heightened interest in the helper becomes apparent: transference. In extreme cases we encounter 'transference neurosis', as a new manifestation of the neurosis. Solution: (1) maintain the transference, as it 'opens up an intermediate region between illness and real life, through which the transition from the former to the latter takes place' (Freud, 1914); and (2) demonstrate how the feelings and actions do not originate in the present situation, so that repetition can be transformed into remembrance and reflection (Freud 1917).[5]

---

[3] The German word '*zärtlich*' is hard to translate, but 'loving' covers it.

[4] Freud seems to use '*erraten*' and '*vermuten*' interchangeably.

[5] In this respect we should mention the fact that 'transference itself is used to overcome transference' (Strachey 1934). In other words, the capacity to analyse transference itself is initially transferential: it is the positive, friendly transference that supports the therapy.

5   Fifth obstacle (after 1905): counter-transference. First described in Freud (1910)[6] as the influence from the patient on the 'unconscious sensing' of the therapist. Solution: Freud (1910) suggested self-analysis and ongoing analysis (i.e. supervision) for the therapist in order to understand and overcome the obstacle so as to be able to return to the work.

6   Sixth obstacle (after 1940, i.e. post-Freud): the therapist's counter-transference keeps bubbling up, even if it is largely understood. Solution: welcoming and using counter-transference as an antenna to deeper listening (Heimann 1950).

Each of these phenomena was 'first considered a somewhat annoying interference with the work, then an instrument of great value, and finally, the main battlefield of treatment' (Racker 1968: 63).

Many people fell by the wayside en route to these discoveries: initially fellow hypnotherapists, then Joseph Breuer in the years after 1890 and then Freud himself (witness the delay in publishing the 'Dora' case). Finally, there was also a distancing from certain earlier Freudian assumptions. This seems to have been a path not just of discovery, but also of a gradually emerging honesty about the discoveries. Freud (1914) himself notes that 'the development of psychoanalytic therapy was probably delayed by a decade at the start, because of an erotic transference situation', obviously a reference to Breuer's treatment of 'Anna O'. Racker (1968) surmises that, perhaps according to some Haeckelian law,[7] this discovery process repeats itself with every new analyst and indeed every new school of psychotherapy, as they struggle initially with defences and resistances, only to become more open about their own counter-transference at a relatively late stage.

Bruchstück einer Hysterie-Analyse (Freud 1905) is the first publication we have that is explicitly about transference. There is only one clear-cut example of transference in the case study that Freud discusses in this paper, related to the first dream: Dora smells 'smoke' just after dreaming. The smoke is linked in the therapy to Freud, but we also learn that Dora's father and Herr K. were passionate smokers as well.[8] Later on, but more implicitly, it seems to be the uninterpreted negative transference which leads to the breakdown of treatment.

In the *Nachwort* (epilogue), which was added almost four years after writing the case study, we find the first definition of transference, and Freud makes a different distinction compared with later years: the one between 'unchanged reprint' and 'revised edition'. This is an important distinction: the first boils down to a primitive displacement of one person by another, and the second has an element of sublimation and adaptation to it which, according to Freud, indicates that the content of the second is

---

[6] Although, as many have pointed out, counter-transference must have been experienced before without being recognised or named as such – e.g. by Breuer in his work with Anna O., or by Freud in his work with 'Dora' (see Lear 2005).

[7] In 1866 the German zoologist Ernst Haeckel proposed that the embryonic development of an individual organism (ontogeny) followed the same path as the evolutionary history of its species (phylogeny).

[8] It is striking that, in this very first book about transference, we find the full triangle-of-person (father, partner and analyst), the Menninger-Malan transference triangle (Malan 1979), all connected around a cigar – the same cigar that has become so associated with Freud himself.

'milder' (Freud 1905). Freud adds that the job of guessing and interpreting transference is the 'hardest' part of the work, as the analyst has to work in a self-reliant manner, with very scant evidence and without getting carried away.[9]

Freud then notes that people will judge this phenomenon as a disadvantage, and perhaps even as evidence that the psychoanalytic cure engenders new pathology. He argues against both positions, stressing first the inevitability of transference and then proposing the converse of his imagined opponent's assertion: 'this, the biggest obstacle of the cure, is destined to become the strongest instrument of it when we succeed to guess it time and time again, and translate it to the patient'.[10]

By the time of the 'Rat Man' case (Freud 1909), Freud shows himself a real master in the field of transference. He demonstrates in some detail how crucial breakthroughs in this treatment happen after he is able to sustain and interpret a heightened negative transference (rude and denigrating abuse directed at Freud combined with existential fear of Freud) and to link the transference to the main discoveries of the treatment so far, after which the Rat Man is able to provide a host of new associations, and improves.

There are fascinating connections between transference and some of Freud's other discoveries: resistance, repetition compulsion and death drive.

Resistance

Resistance is a concept that was introduced by Freud as early as 1895: overcoming resistance takes up much of the *Studien über Hysterie* (Breuer and Freud 1895). Is transference 'resistance', as the phrase 'transference neurosis' (Freud 1914) appears to suggest? Or is transference rather the 'resisted', the relationship that the patient is unable to remember or express, and so does not allow into consciousness (Freud, 1920)? Racker (1968) points to these two contradictory positions that Freud must have held at different times.

Repetition compulsion

Freud introduced repetition compulsion in *Erinnern, Wiederholen und Durcharbeiten* (1914), as something underpinning transference; indeed, in *Jenseits des Lustprinzips* (1920), as something even more fundamental than the pleasure principle. Transference is by definition a repetition, and when it is central to session after session it can well be experienced as a compulsion.

Death drive

In 1920 Freud introduced the term 'death drive', partly as an explanation of negative transference. Before that, he viewed 'love' and 'hate' in the unconscious as very similar, almost interchangeable, as he demonstrates in his dream analysis ('representation by opposites'; Freud 1900). There is good support for the earlier explanation: erotic and

---

[9] I believe this to be the first, veiled reference to counter-transference, a phenomenon that had not yet been named but that Freud experienced strongly with Dora, as we know from other sources.

[10] This is precisely what we try to do in modern supervision, as illustrated by many of the examples in this book.

hostile transference produce very similar obstacles to treatment – so it would seem the death drive is not necessary to grasp the phenomenon of transference.

The different positions taken by Freud can be reconciled by looking at transference as a form of repeating ('being'), rather than remembering ('reflecting on') certain behaviour. This follows on closely from his argument in *Erinnern, Wiederholen und Durcharbeiten* (1914). Transference is then an expression of the unconscious root of our behaviour which springs from earlier experience. When the task is remembering, transference offers resistance to the task. When the task is understanding or interpreting, transference comes across as the 'resisted': the aspects of our being, here and now, that would complete the picture. Transference is not a priori driven in either direction, but is 'always the same' (Freud 1917): that part of us that relates to behaviour elsewhere of which we are not conscious at this moment. It can be an expression of love (Freud 1912), it can be neurosis (Freud 1913) and it can be an expression of hate and self-destructiveness (Freud 1920).

Application and more recent developments

From the earliest days, transference struck Freud and other observers as a form of sublime cooperation and sublime resistance at the same time. Transference is an important phenomenon in psychoanalytic treatment.[11] Other schools of therapy also value the concept, and it has found its way into the world of OD (see e.g. Ledford 1985).

I was first struck by transference in my work in management development in the 1990s. It was our custom to end a workshop with an afternoon working with trained actors. The participants would talk about a recent conversation or an existing relationship that they wanted to improve. The actor would receive brief instructions and then the scene would be played out several times, both according to the original scenario and with new, alternative approaches.

The actors would consistently receive a standing ovation at the end of the afternoon and the participants would remember them as the highlight of the workshop. Many participants remarked on how real the role-play had been for them, how it had felt like being in the room with the real person. It was similarly fascinating to observe the changes in the participants when they were in the scenes, trying to wrestle with their bosses, peers or clients. In supervision and coaching the term 'parallel process' (Searles 1955; Sumerel 1994) is often used to refer to phenomena where both transference and counter-transference play a part. The individual terms are used where one concept is referred to separately.

As an organisation consultant, coach or supervisor, it will be easy to recognise the power of 'transference interpretations': the inescapable and often quite unhinging effect of feedback on here-and-now behaviour as it occurs. A 'stuck' situation can be cut through quickly and effectively, just by bringing to someone's attention how they seem to act or react here and now in this session with you. This is reminiscent of Freud's comment that

---

[11] According to Freud (1917), transference even has the capacity to take over the whole treatment. However, if we read the reports from Freud's patients about his treatment techniques, he rarely appears to address or interpret transference head-on (see Lohser and Newton 1996).

'it is impossible to slay an adversary *in absentia* or in effigy' (Freud 1912; and in different words in Freud 1914). Or, with a single hypothesis about (or even a summary of) the transference here and now, the supervisor can trigger an insight that can cause both the behaviour itself and the underlying issue to disappear like snow in summer.

The phenomenon of transference is discovered only very slowly and carefully, especially because it always involves the discoverer himself. Nowadays we recognise the immediacy of transference and professionals are inclined to see 'parallel processes' everywhere, and especially in the helping relationships they engage in. Freud (1913) also gives an example of immediate-onset transference, namely a patient to whom in the very first session 'nothing' springs to mind, while in reality he is obsessed with the treatment, the consulting room and lying on the couch. Searles (1955: 169) writes:

> My experience in hearing numerous therapists present cases before groups has caused me to become slow in forming an unfavourable opinion of any thera-pist on the basis of his presentation of a case. With convincing frequency I have seen that a therapist who during an occasional presentation appears lamentably anxious, compulsive, confused in his thinking, or what not, actu-ally is a basically capable colleague who, as it were, is trying unconsciously, by this demeanour during the presentation, to show us a major problem-area in the therapy with his patient. This problem area is one that he can neither perceive objectively nor express effectively in words. What he does do is iden-tify with it unconsciously, so that he in fact tries unconsciously to describe it by means of his behaviour as he presents it.

In summary, the importance of transference is not only related to the ubiquity and the immediate onset of the phenomenon, but also to the myriad of possibilities and the complexity of relational patterns that are copied, repeated, partially repeated or mirrored in transference.

Transference is not only 'always the same' (Freud 1917). It is also an immensely rich phenomenon that adapts and transforms itself with repetition – from session to session, and within sessions.

Nowadays the term 'transference resistance' (Freud 1912) is used less and less, in my view, while the emphasis is more on the associative quality of transference. I also suspect that Freud's advice (1913) to leave the theme of transference untouched as long as the patient continues to associate is observed less nowadays, and more therapists feel that transference can be addressed explicitly from day one (Racker 1968).

Here is a brief summary of some more recent influential papers in the area of transference.

- Strachey (1934) looked into the conditions which have to be fulfilled for a transference interpretation to be 'mutative' or effective.
- Heimann (1950), in a short article, advocated reappraising the phenomenon of counter-transference. Heimann and later researchers, including Racker (1968), found that therapists could listen more deeply to the counter-transference they bring to the occasion. They could use their own transferential response to

the patient and the information contained in their own counter-transference for the benefit of the patient.

- Greenson (1965) introduces the concept of the working alliance as a broadening of Freud's concept of *'zärtliche Übertragung'* (friendly transference), which opened up the prospect of actually measuring transference which was followed by the design of psychometric inventories of working alliances. Bordin (1979) made an important contribution by understanding the working alliance in terms of three aspects: agreement on goals; agreement on tasks; and strength of the bond. There is now a plethora of validated instruments, including the Working Alliance Inventory (Horvath and Greenberg 1994), which has also been applied in coaching (e.g. Duckworth *et al.* submitted).

- Searles (1955) made an important new distinction in the phenomena of transference. He pointed out that there are essentially two possibilities: the patient either relives his earlier position (e.g. feeling how it felt with father, acting as he acted with father, etc.) or incorporates the position of the other (e.g. feeling and/or acting like father). He called these two options 'unconscious identification' and 'complementary unconscious identification'. In supervision they are usually termed 'ordinary parallel' and 'reverse parallel' transference respectively (see Chapter 2). Freud must have been aware of this distinction, judging by his analysis of the play of his very young grandson in *Jenseits des Lustprinzips* (Freud 1920), where he describes how the boy takes the role of the 'perpetrator' (his own mother), and thus displays reverse parallel transference from the earlier interaction with his mother.

The still newer, relational school of psychoanalysis also sees transference as a fundamental concept, based on the following.

- The idea that change happens in the relationship, and only in the relationship, leading to the hypothesis that change in the transferential relationship here-and-now is a necessary and perhaps sufficient condition to bring about change outside the consulting room (Stolorow and Atwood 1992).
- The philosophical position that it is not so much libido, as Freud used to think, or our libido objects (Fairbairn 1952) that drive us, as our relationships (Mitchell and Aron 1999) – i.e. our drive to be in relationships that are familiar to us and where we can continue to thrive or suffer in similar ways as experienced before.

Relational psychoanalysis moves the concept of transference right to the centre of personality theory as well as of psychotherapy, where perhaps it should have been all along, since that very first case history of Anna O. in the *Studien über Hysterie* (Breuer and Freud, 1895), were it not for the intricacies of the discovery and revelation process. It is important to note here that many of the innovations that the relational school claims to have introduced are perhaps not as new as advertised, and that much of relational thinking goes all the way back to Freud or at least is not contrary to Freud's theories (Mills 2005).

In summary, it is safe to say that transference has now become completely mainstream in psychotherapy. Therapists, counsellors and supervisors in a wide range of disciplines are now open to a broad spectrum of phenomena in the here and now (during their treatment sessions), ranging from the working alliance to other transferential patterns both as intuited from their clients and as sensed from within themselves. The psychoanalytic literature gives them full encouragement to think about these phenomena and to use them to build what are hopefully effective interpretations.

Conclusions for the start of supervision

Freud (1917) stated that neurotic transference/counter-transference tends to have a rather late onset – i.e. after defences and resistance have already appeared and been recognised as such. He probably didn't mean that transferential phenomena are absent at the start of helping relationships, but that they are not explicitly observed or discussed until later on. Nowadays we recognise the phenomena that Freud described right from the start of helping relationships. It therefore seems worthwhile to investigate if there is perhaps something the supervisor or coach can do to spot transference at an early stage and in any case to make explicit all aspects in himself, including transference. A radical way to do this is to embark on a thought experiment reversing the traditional discovery process. As discussed above, we otherwise run the risk of phenomena occurring along the lines of the traditional discovery process – i.e. that the 'root of the matter' is progressively:

1   avoided altogether
2   hidden in the unconscious
3   defended against
4   buried beneath resistance to the therapy
5   transferred into the therapy room (repeated rather than remembered)
6   obscured by countertransference

In my view, the active reversal of this ontogeny of transferential phenomena has two benefits for the therapist, coach or supervisor. First, he will be better prepared for his sessions as he has already considered his own share in the process. Second, the therapist, coach or supervisor will be literally resisting a process which in itself contributes to the continuation of the problem, as it repeats itself largely unnoticed and so reduces the possibility of new learning or action.

In the following thought experiment, the traditional discovery process is reversed. The therapist, coach or supervisor trains himself, in a way, to become aware of his own counter-transference responses before contracting with a new client. We start with counter-transference and try to notice the other phenomena in reverse order.

6   Racker (1968) suggested that there is a universal counter-transference response which is Oedipal in nature (see Freud 1900 for the 'Oedipus complex'). At the start, countertransference is largely determined by the fact that the supervisor, deep down, wants supervisees of the other sex to adore him and to be superior to

supervisees of the same sex.[12] Not exactly an ideal starting point for a helping relationship, which is precisely why these tendencies were not written about for such a long time and why we need to ponder them carefully before commencing a supervisory relationship. When preparing for a new supervisee or for follow-up sessions, the supervisor can ask himself what instinctual responses he can detect within himself. This can go a bit further than just liking or disliking someone, or experiencing attraction or aversion. The supervisor can easily form a spontaneous 'image' of the supervisee in his mind, even before they have met. Sometimes it is a glance, sometimes a posture, sometimes an action in the room. Words rarely play a role in this picture I form of a supervisee who is still unknown to me. It is more of a sense of being-in-the-room with the other person. Once the supervisor has recognised this feeling, he can analyse it and explore how he is unconsciously preparing for the supervisee: is the supervisor feeling superior, condescending, subservient, anxious, desiring, etc.? Rarely do we feel 'neutral', and if we do there is probably scope for more analysis of that neutrality evidently felt by the supervisor. As the supervisee session draws closer and the supervisor gathers more information and experience, the counter-transferential patterns become more specific. The supervisee will remind the supervisor of someone in particular or will prompt a flurry of emotion in the supervisor with a single gesture. Emotions that the supervisor feels during the sessions have a counter-transferential component. Racker (1968) also describes how some of the supervisor's outlook may change into a 'depressive' one, where his own feelings derive from his own unconscious self-criticism and the supervisor may experience feelings of doubt, inadequacy or superiority with regard to the supervisee. Counter-transference remains important (e.g. as a guide in the event of a perceived rupture in the supervisory relationship). Experienced supervisors are aware that these sorts of disruptions and interferences may turn out to be the main arena of their work. In my case this is true for my own individual supervisees but also for the sponsors of my work and other parties. Time and time again I have noticed that my best and most 'productive' sessions take place soon after an annoying frustration or irritation, assuming of course that the relationship (supervisor–supervisee) survives the conflict.

5   Once the supervisor is somewhat aware of his own counter-transferential response and has analysed at least some of his feelings towards the supervisee, he can begin attending to what the supervisee brings in terms of transference. This quote is apposite here: 'Place yourself on the side of the tendency towards repetition, or on the side of the struggle against the resistances which oppose repetition' (Freud 1920 quoted by Racker 1968: 48). In other words, the supervisor can keep his empathy firmly on the side of the transference in order to understand its origins from within, in particular to understand the supervisee's feelings or ambivalences in so far as they are mirrored in the transference, and to gain an understanding of the (possibly repressed) memory or impulse that has given rise to this particular transference at this particular time. Transference need not be something that develops over time between supervisor and

---

[12] See the observations in Chapter 2 concerning undercurrents within the supervisor–supervisee relationship. These tendencies might well be reversed of course (according to the 'negative Oedipus complex' – Freud, 1923).

supervisee. Like counter-transference, transference starts from session 1 and even before. In my view, it is important that the supervisor should work with transference in a way that is both open-minded and robust – in other words, he should adopt both a thick and a thin skin when responding to transference (de Haan 2008b).

4   Within what the supervisor perceives of the transference towards himself, he tries to identify, name and overcome the resistance of the supervisee from moment to moment. Freud (1912) wrote that 'resistance accompanies treatment on every step' and later (1940) that 'overcoming resistances is that part of the work which causes the most time and the greatest trouble'.[13]

3   While spotting relational phenomena such as counter-transference, transference and resistance, the supervisor continues to practise 'evenly hovering' free association in order to listen to the supervisee both explicitly and implicitly. On this level the information in the supervision session is captured effectively by Malan's 'triangle of conflict' (1979), which includes defences, anxieties and hidden feelings or impulses. Malan argues that the supervisor will notice defences first, as defences form layers of (pre-)consciousness around more hidden anxieties and feelings. Resistance and defence are linked: resistance can be defined as 'defence emerging in the here-and-now relationship' – i.e. as an additional defence needed when the supervisor comes 'too close' in the eyes of the supervisee.

2   By being aware of the context at this moment (including counter-transference, transference and resistance), the supervisor develops the necessary certainty to become more fully aware of the content of the session in this very moment – i.e. what is going on for the supervisee underneath or behind the words spoken, issues and ideas offered and defences demonstrated. We can regard defences as a layer of protection, insulation and/or dampening of *anxiety*, which thus becomes the supervisor's next discovery in his journey of understanding.

1   Finally, anxiety can be seen as a consequence of an emerging wish or feeling that is ambivalent, problematic or unwelcome. This deep feeling or impulse lies at the root of the perspectives that went before, and will only be discovered last as the supervisor gains a better understanding of the relationship here and now, and of resistances, defences and anxiety.

The figure overleaf outlines the various aspects of (or perspectives on) the here-and-now in a supervision session, without seeking to reify any of these aspects. Each of the six concepts may describe the same affect or emotion during a session, from various viewpoints. In addition, the six concepts amount essentially to one and the same 'thing', namely the thing that is going on at this moment, which could be called the 'issue' or the 'symptom' as it presents itself right now. These various perspectives, or ways the issue engages with the supervisor, are ever-present and are themselves multi-layered, ambiguous and contradictory. Of these six, resistance is probably the one that

---

[13] Within the context of this appendix it is relevant to note that, in the last technical introduction that Freud wrote in his last year in London, but left unfinished, he follows the same order as here: he covers transference first and then moves on to resistance as the 'other important part of our job' (Freud 1940), while in his earlier, more historically based overview (Freud 1917), resistance comes first.

is most 'objective' or best observable. The others are usually hidden below the surface to various degrees.

The figure is an attempt to depict in graphic form how counter-transference may be an entry point for an understanding of the other person, via transference, resistance, etc. The figure contains:

- Three relational perspectives on the supervision here and now:
    CT: countertransference
    T: transference
    R: resistance
- Three more subjective perspectives on the supervision here and now:
    D: defence
    A: anxiety
    F: hidden feeling or impulse

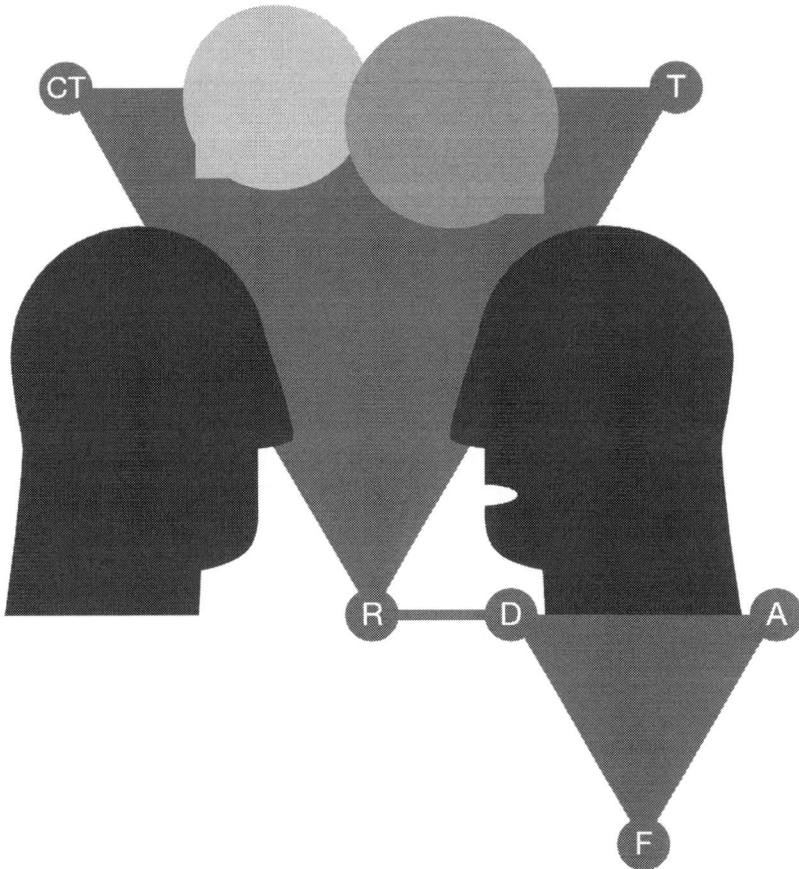

An overview of the six 'stages of discovery' or psychodynamic characteristics that inform the phenomenon of transference, building on Malan's triangle of conflict (1979).

Appendix B: The relational approach and quantitative research

In this appendix I attempt once and for all to answer the questions that (should) concern all supervisors most in our practice:

1   What should we say and do at any moment in supervision in order to maximise our effectiveness?
2   How should we help our supervisees to achieve all of their supervision objectives?
3   How do we ensure that our supervisees and their sponsors keep coming back to us when they need more supervision?

The answers to these three questions are like the three wishes offered by the proverbial good fairy to some lucky supervisor. Wouldn't the supervisor's life be utterly complete and worthwhile if he could just find a definitive and satisfactory answer to all three questions, say by reading just one appendix in a book on supervision? Unfortunately, a supervisor's life is too complicated, ambiguous and uncertain for that, and that is perhaps what makes our field so rich and enjoyable. It is my firm conviction that we cannot give any strict dos and don'ts. What we *can* do, in my view, is take the research literature carefully and critically to heart. By listening as objectively as possible to what our own supervisees – or similar assignments of other supervisors – tell us, we can perhaps, with a lot of difficulty and effort, take tiny steps towards answering those three questions for ourselves. Just like our supervisees, we learn by taking a careful and critical look at our own practice, gradually becoming better informed and more professional in the process. I myself see no other way to do this than by sound and rigorous research.

Here I give a brief summary of the state of current research into effectiveness within supervision, executive coaching and psychotherapy. But I should add that there has not been much empirical research to date into the effectiveness of supervision, and none at all as far as I could ascertain into the effectiveness of supervision for coaches and organisation consultants. Empirical research in the fields of supervision and coaching is not yet advanced enough, in my opinion, to allow any firm conclusions on effectiveness, while research in psychotherapy has a much longer tradition and has indeed produced undisputed results. I will summarise the latter research with my '10 commandments for the supervisor' (as in de Haan 2008a). As I will show, the initial results of quantitative research into executive coaching appear to confirm these results in psychotherapy.

For convenience, I assume in this appendix that similar factors are at play in supervision, coaching and psychotherapy. This is a crucial assumption for which I have little evidence apart from my personal experience as a supervisor, coach and psychotherapist, and similar experiences of colleagues working in all three disciplines.

Little is known as yet about the effectiveness of coaching and supervision

Outside the field of organisation consulting and coaching, we find strong evidence of the effectiveness of supervision for social workers and nurses among others. Bradshaw *et al.* (2007) show that trainee psychiatric nurses have a wider knowledge of interventions if they undergo regular supervision by a more experienced colleague. In addition, their clients (psychiatric patients) appear to experience a more marked reduction in symptoms than clients of nurses who do not take part in such workplace supervision.

A comprehensive meta-analysis of 27 studies (Mor Barak *et al.* 2009) covering a total of 10,867 social workers showed that each of three aspects of supervision ('assistance with tasks', 'social and emotional support' and 'interpersonal interaction') correlates positively with aspects such as effectiveness, satisfaction, length of time in position, commitment and psychological well-being of social workers. These are encouraging results but we don't know how relevant they are to the supervision of consultants and coaches, who work in a completely different context and generally have a much lower frequency of supervision.[1]

The empirical literature within executive coaching offers only a small number of thorough quantitative studies into effectiveness – every reason to study and summarise them carefully, especially since we also look at this practice in coaching supervision sessions. The following is a summary of my own knowledge of this literature.

A substantial proportion of research articles look at the value of coaching from the perspective of the client. For example, clients are asked to estimate how much their coaching has contributed to the bottom line of their organisation in financial terms (see McGovern *et al.* 2001). This type of article does not meet the requirements of modern quantitative research, such as objective measurement criteria and comparison with a (randomly selected) control group. I found only seven studies which explore the effectiveness of coaching on the basis of criteria other than client satisfaction (four of which failed to employ a control group). Olivero *et al.* (1997) studied managers who had taken part in a three-day training programme followed by eight weeks of coaching. They found that both the training and the coaching increased productivity considerably, with the bulk of the increase attributable to the coaching. In a study by Thach (2002), managers underwent a 360° feedback process before and after their coaching. There was

---

[1] Lawton (2000) stresses in this connection that most research in the field of supervision has taken place in a training context – i.e. not in a situation where supervisor and supervisee are more or less equal in terms of seniority, as is often the case with consultants and coaches.

an average increase in 'leadership effectiveness', both in terms of managers' self-perception as well as perception by others.

Significant effects as a result of executive coaching were also found by Peterson (1993) and as a result of mentoring by Ragins *et al.* (2000). The latter studied 1162 professionals from a variety of organisations to determine the extent to which formal or informal mentoring relationships[2] influenced their attitudes to their work and careers. Of these, 44 per cent of the respondents had an informal mentor, 9 per cent had a formal mentor as part of a mentoring programme and 47 per cent had no mentor (the control group). In this study, client satisfaction with the mentoring relationship proved to be the decisive factor in terms of effectiveness. Without that satisfaction, there were no demonstrable differences between professionals who did and did not have a mentor. Satisfied professionals were found to be much more positive about themselves (self-confidence), their work, promotion chances, organisation and career; no significant difference was found between formal and informal mentoring. Evers *et al.* (2006) measured self-efficacy beliefs and outcome expectancies on each of three dimensions. Their study compared a pre-intervention and post-intervention measurement and also involved a control group. Although their sample was not very large (30 managers in both the experimental and the control group), they did find significant evidence for a positive effect of the coaching sessions: on one of the three dimensions, the coached group scored significantly higher than the control group, in terms of both self-efficacy beliefs ('setting one's own goals') and outcome expectancies ('acting in a balanced way').

One of the most thorough studies into the impact of executive coaching was undertaken by Smither *et al.* (2003). This study involved a control group, evaluations by independent researchers and by the clients' superiors, colleagues and staff (360° feedback). In short, a more objective criterion than the opinions of clients themselves, which Peterson (1993) and Ragins *et al.* (2000) took as their basis. Smither *et al.* looked at two consecutive years of 360° feedback for 1202 senior managers in a multinational organisation. The researchers found that managers who worked with an executive coach are significantly more likely than other managers to set specific goals, solicit suggestions from their superiors and obtain higher ratings from direct reports and superiors.

In the small but growing body of literature on coaching outcomes, I also found six articles exploring the question of *what sort* of coaching is effective. This research concerns the 'active ingredients' of coaching: which coaching models, qualities of coaches or coaching behaviours make a difference for clients?

Scoular and Linley (2006) looked at (1) how the helpfulness experienced was influenced by setting goals explicitly at the beginning of the conversation; and (2) how the perceived effectiveness was influenced by personality (dis-)similarities between coach and client, as measured by the Myers-Briggs Temperament Indicator (MBTI). The effect

---

[2] For an overview of other studies in the field of mentoring, see the meta-analysis in Allen *et al.* (2004), with 43 effect studies in the organisational domain, including Ragins *et al.* (2000). This meta-analysis found consistently small but significant and positive effects of mentoring on, among other things, promotions and career satisfaction. Allen *et al.* (2004) also found that satisfaction with the mentoring relationship is the best predictor of career outcomes.

measurements two and eight weeks after a single short coaching session showed no difference between 'goal-setting' and 'no goal-setting'. However, it was found that the outcome scores were significantly higher the more the coach and client differed in terms of personality.

Stewart *et al.* (2008) looked at how well the personality (measured on the 'big five' personality factors – see Digman 1990) and 'self-efficacy' (Schwarzer *et al.* 1999) of the client predicted coaching outcome. These client factors were correlated with coaching outcomes for 110 coaching clients. Moderate positive effects were found for conscientiousness, openness, emotional stability and general self-efficacy, but the authors warn that other personality factors are likely to play a role as well.

Boyce *et al.* (2010) studied 74 coach–client relationships in the context of a US military academy, where clients were cadets and coaches were senior military leaders who had had some training in executive coaching. The study analysed the impact of relationship factors (such as rapport, trust and commitment) and matching factors (such as demographic commonality, behavioural compatibility and coach reputation) on coaching outcome. They found that matching had no significant impact on outcome, while the quality of the coaching relationship was indeed significant, explaining as much as 50 per cent of the variance when scored by clients and 25 per cent when scored by coaches. Very similar results were found by Duckworth *et al.* (submitted) with a sample of 131 coach–client relationships from various organisations.

With another sample of 30 internal coaching relationships linked to a leadership development programme within a manufacturing company, Baron and Morin (2009) and Baron *et al.* (2011) were able to show that working alliance as a relationship factor (as measured using the Working Alliance Inventory – see Horvath and Greenberg 1994) predicted coaching outcomes significantly, provided they were rated by clients, not when rated by coaches.

De Haan *et al.* (2011) examined how various executive coaching interventions make a difference to clients. Seventy-one coaching clients (from different organisations) reported on the frequency and influence of coaches' interventions. The researchers found no demonstrable distinction between specific coaching interventions, leading to the conclusion that the extent to which coaching is experienced as helpful depends not on the technique or approach chosen but more on factors that are common to all forms of coaching, such as the relationship, empathy, expectation, etc.

In summary, research into coaching outcomes is clearly still in its infancy and the holy grail of the executive coaching outcome is still there to be sought. There is no generally accepted standard, such as the randomised controlled trials in psychotherapeutic research (Wampold 2001). What is also striking is that the first four research papers mentioned above (Peterson 1993; Olivero *et al.* 1997; McGovern *et al.* 2001; Thach 2002), which did not use a control group, found very large effects (much larger than those found in psychotherapy), while the three more rigorous studies with a control group discussed next (Ragins *et al.* 2000; Smither *et al.* 2003; Evers *et al.* 2006) found only small effects (smaller than those found in psychotherapy). It seems that, if the experience of the client alone is measured, the outcome tends to be positive. The effect is much smaller, but still positive, if more objective standards are used.

Translating findings from psychotherapy: the 10 commandments

The articles on different coaching interventions which are discussed above (Scoular and Linley, 2006; Stewart *et al.* 2008; Baron and Morin 2009; Boyce *et al.* 2010; de Haan *et al.* 2011; Duckworth *et al.* submitted) clearly show a pattern that corresponds to the findings in psychotherapy, namely that common factors such as personality, rapport/working alliance and self-efficacy have a significant positive relationship with the outcome of coaching.

In short, researchers studying the effectiveness of psychotherapy have found the following answers.

- *Does psychotherapy have an effect?* Yes, because the client of psychotherapy does demonstrably better on average than 80 per cent of the control group (Wampold 2001). In the social and medical sciences this is regarded as a 'large effect'.
- *Which aspects of psychotherapy have an effect?* Not the differences in intervention, technique, approach, model or protocol, but aspects that play a role in every approach (common factors), such as the client context, the structure and context of the sessions, the personality of the therapist and the relationship between client and therapist (Cooper 2008).
- *Under what conditions do demonstrable effects occur?* We know very little about this as yet, but there are strong indications that the therapist's trust in his approach and the client's expectations are more important than previously thought (Wampold 2001).

Research into the results of psychotherapy normally uses an effect size d, which is the difference between the means of two distributions on a standardised scale, mostly success rates of group 1 (patients) and success rates of group 2 (control group). An effect greater than $d \approx 0.80$ is termed a 'large effect', between $d \approx 0.50$ and 0.80 is a 'medium effect' and less than $d \approx 0.20$ is a 'small effect'. The main findings of meta-analytical research in psychotherapy are as follows (for more information, see de Haan 2008a).

- Psychotherapy is highly effective (effect size $d \approx 0.85$).
- There is a negligible difference in effectiveness between each pair of different approaches (effect $d < 0.20$).
- The active ingredients of therapy are therefore common to many approaches:
  - relationship-related factors: working alliance, commitment, transference;
  - client-related factors: hope of change, motivation, problem pressure;
  - therapist-related factors: personal traits, cultivation of positive expectations, warmth, appreciation, attention;
  - change-related factors: opportunity for expression, practice and acquiring a rationale for change;
  - structure-related factors: use of techniques or rituals, exploration of issues the patient is struggling with and commitment to a particular model or method;

   – external factors: help from friends and family, changes occurring independently of the therapy.

The strongest of these 'common factors' are:

* the quality of the relationship (working alliance as rated by the client): $d \approx$
  0.54;
* the person of the therapist: $0.50 < d < 0.65$;
* the client: the least-studied but probably the most effective factor in therapy
  – well-founded estimates put the effect of 'hope' at $d \approx 0.85$ and that of the
  influence of external factors in the life of the client at $d \approx 1.65$ (Lambert 1992).

Based on these meta-analyses in psychotherapy, I proposed the following '10 commandments' for the executive coach and supervisor in my book *Relational Coaching* (de Haan
2008a).

1 First, do no harm

This first commandment might appear self-evident but, given some reports of abuse in
executive coaching (Berglas 2002), is perhaps not entirely superfluous. Moreover, it has
been demonstrated that therapeutic methods have less effect if they are used non-
therapeutically but, say, as a way of passing the time or in order to create a 'stationary'
control group (see Wampold 2001). The conclusion often drawn in medicine from this
principle (*primum non nocere*) is *in dubio abstine* – i.e. if in doubt, it is better to do nothing
than do something that may harm the supervisee/client.

2 Have confidence

A coach/supervisor who follows tried and tested ethical principles and tries honestly to
help the client/supervisee stands a good chance of succeeding. By all accounts, helping
interventions are highly effective. You are not necessarily any better at it than other
coaches or supervisors (an illusion that is easily acquired, however, in the isolation of
your sessions), but you stand a good chance of doing it more or less as well as they do.

3 Commit yourself heart and soul to your approach

No one method is demonstrably better than any other. However, it *has* been shown
that effectiveness is increased if the therapist expressly adopts a particular professional
approach from which his interventions are derived, provided that choice is honest and
intended to help the client. In other words, commit yourself heart and soul to your
approach but resist the temptation to believe that it is intrinsically superior.

4 Feed the hope of your supervisee

Hope is such an important factor for effectiveness in therapy (Lambert 1992) that it
would be a mistake for a coach/supervisor to do anything to undermine it. Your initial

response to supervisees' doubts ('Will this help me?', 'What will five supervision sessions give me?') is possibly also the worst one: 'I don't know yet. I have no idea if this will help you.' With that answer you run the risk, in all honesty and openness, of undermining that valuable hope in your supervisee. It is better to remain hopeful yourself and respond, equally truthfully, that 'Supervision has helped many other people with similar issues'; or 'I have positive expectations that we can achieve a lot in every session'.

5 Consider the supervisory situation from your supervisee's perspective

All the signs are that it is primarily the supervisee's view on things that determines how effective a given supervision journey will be. What is important, therefore, is how your supervisee sees you and experiences the working alliance with you, so collect as much feedback from your supervisees as you can.

6 Work on your supervisory relationship

Coaching and supervision are not just about the supervisee and his issues, or the supervisee's clients, their issues and their organisations; they are mainly about the relationship. A good relationship holds out better prospects of change for the better, even if issues are not fully addressed. So pay attention to your relationship and the quality of your working alliance with your supervisee, and make it explicit if that helps to make it stronger. Avoid interventions that needlessly jeopardise the working alliance with the supervisee.

7 If you don't 'click', find another supervisor

The working relationship between coach/supervisor and client/supervisee is perhaps the most important success factor. If the relationship is poor, other important success factors, such as the above-mentioned expectations of the supervisee, will suffer as a result. In addition, as in psychotherapy, we can expect the bulk of any achievements to be made in the first few sessions. If that part is already under pressure, it is better to 'regain' this and other success factors by bringing in a different supervisor. Luborsky (1976) suggests doing this as soon as the problem becomes apparent. Miller *et al.* (2006) achieved higher effect scores in psychotherapy by constantly monitoring the working alliance as perceived by the client and suggesting a change of therapist in the event of a working alliance that was less than ideal. But be aware that a referral to another supervisor also puts the relationship under pressure. The supervisee always experiences a referral partly as a rejection and a loss, however much he understands that it is better to move forward with someone else. So refer carefully and helpfully, and remain available to the supervisee for any questions or further conversations.

8 Look after yourself and your well-being

It is not even just about the issue, the supervisee, the supervisee's clients, their organisations and the relationship; supervision is also about your own personality, or in any case your personality as perceived by the supervisee. It therefore helps to know how you are seen by others. Make sure you are seen as someone who 'helps' others in one way or another. How this translates into character traits is not very clear as yet, but it seems to help if the therapist comes across as attractive, competent, stable, healthy, happy, empathetic, warm and trustworthy.

9 Try to stay fresh and unbiased

Applying predetermined procedures and protocols, however ingenious and carefully chosen, appears to have little influence on the outcome of supervision. Quite the contrary. Supervisors who meet the supervisee with a fresh, unbiased and sympathetic approach, and thus pay more attention to the supervisee's situation and their relationship with the supervisee, appear to be more effective.

10 Don't worry too much about the specific things you are doing

According to the meta-analyses (Wampold 2001), specific methods and techniques are much less relevant to the final outcome than the general success factors mentioned above – and there are even strong indications that specific interventions make no difference at all. Clients who are subsequently asked to name the most effective ingredients of their therapy journey very rarely mention specific moments or interventions, and much more often the personality of the therapist or the opportunity to talk to someone who understands and supports them (see Tallman and Bohart 1999). Knowing that it is not about the specific things you say or do during sessions can make you more self-assured and more relaxed as a supervisor. For example, it doesn't seem so terrible if you say the wrong thing or forget relevant comments from previous sessions. You learn to pay more attention to what is actually going on here and now in this supervisory relationship.

The relational approach in supervision

After studying the meta-analyses in psychotherapy, I find that many guidelines for supervisors place too much emphasis on the supervisor and on specific interventions, structures and methods. As a consequence, I have devoted part of this book explicitly to the supervisee (Chapter 3) and co-wrote Chapter 5 with one of my supervisees. The recent findings in psychotherapy outcome research are both sobering and illuminating. If we use these findings as inspiration in supervision, we should place much less emphasis on our knowledge as supervisors and instead look primarily at our relationship with the supervisee and what is going on in that relationship.

Supervision is mainly about the supervisee trying to understand and change himself and his practice. It is much easier for the supervisee to do this than for the supervisor to achieve something directly with a carefully thought-out choice of interventions. The supervisee in fact does it all himself. The supervisor only helps the supervisee to identify and activate his naturally inherent capabilities. We know how important supervision can be for our supervisees and how effective supervision sessions can be, but we should be aware who is actually doing the work: the supervisee!

The 10 commandments given above lead to a supervisory approach that can be termed 'relational supervision', following on from a therapeutic tradition in psychoanalysis (see Mitchell 1988) and other schools. This approach assumes that the most important active ingredient that the supervisor can influence during the sessions in order to achieve the best possible outcome of supervision is the relationship with the supervisee.

Relational supervision is a philosophy where both supervisee and supervisor:

- attempt to understand the material contributed by the supervisee from the angle of the relationships within and surrounding the case material – all content of supervision can be regarded as relational;
- endeavour to build a relationship that is as strong and productive as possible – the working alliance is what counts;
- devote attention to the developing relationship as a mirror of, or laboratory for, the supervisee developing his client relationships;
- do not deny themselves any specific interventions, regarding either the nature or the sequence of contributions; if the supervisor believes that a particular intervention suits his own personality, and can fully support it, without conflict with accepted ethical codes, then that choice is justified.

All of these aspects of relational supervision work together to make the supervisee and the supervisory relationship (as it develops from moment to moment) as central as possible in the supervision session, in the interest of clients, supervisees and their organisations. All of this means that the relational supervisor pays constant attention to what is going on in the relationship with his supervisee.

A warning is appropriate at this point, however. The research results from the meta-analyses do not justify the adoption of an eclectic, pluralistic or 'nihilistic' attitude. The research results tell us that any existing professional approach is as good as any other, but they *don't* tell us that we can exchange or combine approaches as we please, or that we can disregard the approaches themselves and their importance. The effectiveness of therapy, coaching or supervision appears to depend largely on the adoption and application of a preferred approach. An eclectic, pluralistic or nihilistic supervisor might feel all too free to combine approaches, methods and ideologies as his fancy takes him – i.e. not to have a preferred approach at all. Such a supervisor runs the risk of piling intervention on intervention at random, without considering reflectively how they fit in with his own ideology or his own understanding of the objectives of this relationship.

References

Allen, T.D., Eby, L.T., Poteet, M.L., Lentz, E. and Lima, L. (2004) Career benefits associated with mentoring for protégés: a meta-analysis, *Journal of Applied Psychology*, 89: 127–36.

Andersen, S. and Berk, M.S. (1998) The social-cognitive model of transference: experiencing past relationships in the present, *Current directions in Psychological Science*, 7(4): 109–15.

Asch, S.E. (1951) Effects of group pressure upon the modification and distortion of judgments, in H. Guetzkow (ed.) *Groups, Leadership and Men*. Pittsburgh, PA: Carnegie Press.

Atkinson, T. and Claxton, G. (2000) *The Intuitive Practitioner*. Buckingham: Open University Press.

Bachkirova, T., Jackson, P. and Clutterbuck, D. (eds) (2011) *Coaching & Mentoring Supervision: Theory and Practice*. Maidenhead: Open University Press.

Baron, L. and Morin, L. (2009) The coach–coachee relationship in executive coaching: a field study, *Human Resource Development Quarterly*, 20(1): 85–106.

Baron, L., Morin, L. and Morin, D. (2012) Executive coaching: the effect of working alliance discrepancy on the development of coachees' self-efficacy, in E. de Haan and C. Sills (eds) *Coaching Relationships*. Faringdon: Libri.

Berglas, S. (2002) The very real dangers of executive coaching, *Harvard Business Review*, June: 86–92.

Bion, W.R. (1961) *Experiences in Groups*. London: Tavistock.

Bion, W.R. (1962) *Learning from Experience*. London: Heinemann.

Bion, W.R. (1963) *Elements of Psychoanalysis*. London: Heinemann.

Bion, W.R. (1970) *Attention and Interpretation*. London: Tavistock.

Bion, W.R. (1973/1974) *Brazilian Lectures* (published in 1990). London: Karnac.

Bordin, H. (1979) The generalizability of the psychoanalytic concept of the working alliance, *Psychotherapy: Theory, Research and Practice*, 16: 252–60.

Boyce, L.A., Jackson, R.J. and Neal, L.J. (2010) Building successful leadership coaching relationships: examining impact of matching criteria in a leadership coaching program, *Journal of Management Development*, 29(10): 914–31.

Bradshaw T., Butterworth, A. and Mairs, H. (2007) Does structured clinical supervision during psychosocial intervention education enhance outcome for mental health nurses and the service users they work with? *Journal of Psychiatric and Mental Health Nursing*, 14: 4–12.

Breuer, J. and Freud, S. (1895) *Studien über Hysterie*. Leipzig: Verlag Franz Deuticke. Translated as *Studies on Hysteria* by James Strachey in collaboration with Anna Freud in *The Standard Edition of the Complete Psychological Works of Sigmund Freud*, vol. II.

Brounstein, M. (2000) *Coaching and Mentoring for Dummies*. New York: Wiley.

Carroll, M. (2009) From mindless to mindful practice: on learning reflection in supervision, *Psychotherapy in Australia*, 15(4): 40–51.

Carroll, M. (2010) Levels of reflection: on learning reflection, *Psychotherapy in Australia*, 16(2): 28–35.

Carroll, M. and Gilbert, M. (2005) *On Becoming a Supervisee: Creating Learning Partnerships.* London: Vukani.

Casement, P. (2002) *Learning from our Mistakes.* London: Routledge.

Cooper, M. (2008) *Essential Research Findings in Counselling and Psychotherapy – The Facts Are Friendly.* London: Sage.

Cunningham, I. (1994) *The Wisdom of Strategic Learning – The Self Managed Learning Solution.* Maidenhead: McGraw-Hill.

Day, A., De Haan, E., Blass, E., Sills, C. and Bertie, C. (2008) Coaches' experience of critical moments in the coaching, *International Coaching Psychology Review*, 3(3): 207–18.

de Haan, E. (2004) *Learning With Colleagues – An Action Guide to Action Learning.* Basingstoke: Palgrave Macmillan.

de Haan, E. (2006) *Fearless Consulting – Temptations, Risks and Limits of the Profession.* Chichester: Wiley.

de Haan, E. (2008a) *Relational Coaching – Journeys Towards Mastering One-to-one Learning.* Chichester: Wiley.

de Haan, E. (2008b) Becoming simultaneously thicker and thinner skinned: the inherent conflicts arising in the professional development of coaches, *Personnel Review*, 37(5): 526–42.

de Haan, E. and Burger, Y. (2005) *Coaching with Colleagues – An Action Guide to One-to-one Learning.* Basingstoke: Palgrave Macmillan.

de Haan, E., Curd, J. and Culpin, V. (2011) Executive coaching in practice: what determines helpfulness for clients of coaching? *Personnel Review*, 40(1): 24–44.

Digman, J.M. (1990) Personality structure: emergence of the Five Factor Model, *Annual Review of Psychology*, 41: 417–40.

Doehrman, M.J. (1976) Parallel processes in supervision and psychotherapy, *Bulletin of the Menninger Clinic*, 40: 1–104.

Duckworth, A., de Haan, E., Birch, D., Hardman P. and Jones, C. (submitted) Executive coaching outcome research: the contribution of common factors such as relationship, personality match and self-efficacy, *Consulting Psychology Journal: Practice and Research*.

Evers, W.J.G., Brouwers, A. and Tomic, W. (2006) A quasi-experimental study on management coaching effectiveness, *Consulting Psychology Journal: Practice and Research*, 58: 174–82.

Fairbairn, W.R.D. (1952) *Psychoanalytic Studies of the Personality.* London: Tavistock.

Fine, C. (2007). *A Mind of its Own – How the Brain Distorts and Deceives.* Cambridge: Icon Books.

Fivush, R. and Neisser, U. (1994) *The Remembering Self: Construction and Accuracy in the Self-narrative.* New York: Cambridge University Press.

Fliess, R. (1942) The metapsychology of the analyst, *Psychoanalytic Quarterly*, 11: 211–27.

Fonagy, P., Steele, M., Steele, H., Higgitt, A.C. and Target, M. (1994) Theory and practice of resilience, *Journal of Child Psychology and Psychiatry*, 35: 231–57.

Foucault, M. (1982) Technologies of the self: a seminar with Michel Foucault, in L.H. Martin, H. Gutman and P.H. Hutton (eds) *Technologies of the Self: A Seminar with Michel Foucault.* Amherst, MA: University of Massachusetts Press (1988).

Freud, S. (1900) *Die Traumdeutung.* Vienna: Verlag Franz Deuticke. Translated as *The Interpretation of Dreams* by James Strachey in collaboration with Anna Freud in *The Standard Edition of the Complete Psychological Works of Sigmund Freud*, vols IV and V. London: Hogarth.

Freud, S. ([1904] 1924) *Zur psychopathologie des Alltagslebens: 10. Weiter vermehrte Auflage.* Vienna: Internationale Psychoanalytische Verlag. Translated as *The Psychopathology of Everyday Life* by James Strachey in collaboration with Anna Freud in *The Standard Edition of the Complete Psychological Works of Sigmund Freud*, vol. VI. London: Hogarth.

Freud, S. (1905) *Bruchstück einer Hysterie-Analyse. Monatsschrift für Psychiatrie und Neurologie*, vol. XXVIII, Book 4. Translated as *Fragment of an Analysis of a Case of Hysteria* by James Strachey in collaboration with Anna Freud in *The Standard Edition of the Complete Psychological Works of Sigmund Freud*, vol. VII. London: Hogarth.

Freud, S. (1909) *Bemerkungen über einen Fall von Zwangsneurose. Jahrbuch für psychoanalytische und psychopathologische Forschungen*, Band I. Leipzig/Vienna: Verlag Franz Deuticke. Translated as *Notes on a Case of Obsessional Neurosis* by James Strachey in collaboration with Anna Freud in *The Standard Edition of the Complete Psychological Works of Sigmund Freud*, vol. X. London: Hogarth.

Freud, S. (1910). *Die zukünftigen Chancen der psychoanalytischen Therapie. Zentralblatt für Psychoanalyse*, Band I. Translated as *The Future Prospects of Psycho-analytic Therapy* by James Strachey in collaboration with Anna Freud in *The Standard Edition of the Complete Psychological Works of Sigmund Freud*, vol. XI. London: Hogarth.

Freud, S. (1912) *Zur Dynamik der Übertragung, Zentralblatt für Psychoanalyse*, vol. II. Translated as *The Dynamics of Transference* by James Strachey in collaboration with Anna Freud in *The Standard Edition of the Complete Psychological Works of Sigmund Freud*, vol. XI. London: Hogarth.

Freud, S. (1913) *Zur Einleitung der Behandlung. Internationale Zeitschrift für ärztliche Psychoanalyse*, vol. I. Translated as *On Beginning the Treatment* by James Strachey in collaboration with Anna Freud in *The Standard Edition of the Complete Psychological Works of Sigmund Freud*, vol. XII. London: Hogarth.

Freud, S. (1914) *Erinnern, Wiederholen und Durcharbeiten. Zeitschrift für Psychoanalyse*, vol. II. Translated as *Remembering, Repeating and Working Through* by James Strachey in collaboration with Anna Freud in *The Standard Edition of the Complete Psychological Works of Sigmund Freud*, vol. XII. London: Hogarth.

Freud, S. (1915) *Bemerkungen über die Übertragungsliebe. Zeitschrift für Psychoanalyse*, vol. III. Translated as *Observations on Transference-Love* by James Strachey in collaboration with Anna Freud in *The Standard Edition of the Complete Psychological Works of Sigmund Freud*, vol. XIII. London: Hogarth.

Freud, S. (1917) *Vorlesungen zur Einführung in die Psychoanalyse, XXVII. Vorlesung: Die Übertragung.* Leipzig: Verlag Hugo Heller. Translated as *Introductory Lectures on Psychoanalysis, XVII: Transference* by James Strachey in collaboration with Anna Freud in *The Standard Edition of the Complete Psychological Works of Sigmund Freud*, vol. XVI. London: Hogarth.

Freud, S. (1920). *Jenseits des Lustprinzips.* Leipzig/Vienna/Zürich: Internationaler Psychoanalytischer Verlag. Translated as *Beyond the Pleasure Principle* by James Strachey in collaboration with Anna Freud in *The Standard Edition of the Complete Psychological Works of Sigmund Freud*, vol. XVIII. London: Hogarth.

Freud, S. (1923). *Das Ich und das Es.* Leipzig/Vienna/Zürich: Internationaler psychoanalytischer Verlag. Translated as *The Ego and the Id* by James Strachey in collaboration with Anna Freud in *The Standard Edition of the Complete Psychological Works of Sigmund Freud*, vol. XIX. London: Hogarth.

Freud, S. (1940) *Abriss der Psychoanalyse. Internationale Zeitschrift für Psychoanalyse und Imago*. Translated as *An Outline of Psycho-analysis* by James Strachey in collaboration with Anna Freud in *The Standard Edition of the Complete Psychological Works of Sigmund Freud*, vol. XXIII. London: Hogarth.

Garvin, D.A. (2000) *Learning in Action*. Boston, MA: Harvard Business School Press.

Goodman, G.S., Magnussen, S., Andersson, J., Endestad, T., Løkke, C. and Mostue, C. (2006) Memory illusions and false memories in real life, in S. Magnussen and T. Helstrup (eds) *Everyday Memory*. Hove: Psychology Press.

Gray, L.A., Ladany, N., Walker, J.A. and Ancis, J.R. (2001) Psychotherapy trainees' experience of counterproductive events in supervision, *Journal of Counselling Psychology*, 48: 371–83.

Greenson, R.R. (1965) The working alliance and the transference neuroses, *Psychoanalysis Quarterly*, 34: 155–81.

Haeckel, E. (1866) *Generale Morphologie der Organismen [General morphology]*. Berlin: Verlag von Georg Reimer.

Harrison, R. (1997) A time for letting go, *Organization Development Journal*, 15(2): 79–86.

Hawkins, P. and Shohet, R. (2006) *Supervision in the Helping Professions*, 3rd edn. Maidenhead: Open University Press.

Hawkins, P. and Smith, N. (2006) *Coaching, Mentoring and Organizational Consultancy: Supervision and Development*. Maidenhead: Open University Press.

Hawthorne, L. (1975) Games supervisors play, *Social Work*, 20(3): 179–83.

Heimann, P. (1950) On counter-transference, *International Journal of Psychoanalysis*, 31: 81–4.

Hirschhorn, L. (1988) *The Workplace Within – Psychodynamics Of Organizational Life*. Cambridge, MA: MIT Press.

Horvath, A.O. and Greenberg, L.S. (eds) (1994) *The Working Alliance: Theory, Research and Practice*. New York: Wiley.

Kadushin, A. (1968) Games people play in supervision, *Social Work*, 13(3): 23–32.

Kadushin, A. (1976) *Supervision in Social Work*. New York: Columbia University Press.

Klein, M. (1946) Notes on some schizoid mechanisms, *International Journal of Psychoanalysis*, 27(3).

Kolb, D.A. (1984) *Experiential Learning – Experience as the Source of Learning and Development*. Englewood Cliffs, NJ: Prentice Hall.

Kraus, M.W. and Chen, S. (2010) Facial-feature resemblance elicits the transference effect, *Psychological Science*, 21: 518–22.

Kutzik, A.J. (1977a) The medical field, in F.W. Kaslow *et al.* (eds) *Supervision, Consultation, and Staff Training in the Helping Professions*. San Francisco: Jossey-Bass.

Kutzik, A.J. (1977b) The social work field, in F.W. Kaslow *et al.* (eds) *Supervision, Consultation, and Staff Training in the Helping Professions*. San Francisco: Jossey-Bass.

Lambert (1992) Psychotherapy outcome research, in J.C. Norcross and M.R. Goldfried (eds) *Handbook of Psychotherapy Integration*. New York: Basic Books.

Lawton, B. (2000) 'A very exposing affair': explorations in counsellors' supervisory relationships, in B. Lawton and C. Feltham (eds) *Taking Supervision Forward: Enquiries and Trends in Counselling and Psychotherapy*. London: Sage.

Lear, J. (2005) *Freud*. Abingdon: Routledge.

Ledford, G.E. Jr (1985) Transference and countertransference in action research relationships, *Consultation*, 4(1): 36–51.

Lehrer, J. (2009) *The Decisive Moment: How the Brain Makes Up Its Mind*. London: Canongate.

Lohser, B. and Newton, P.M. (1996) *Unorthodox Freud – The View From the Couch*. New York: The Guilford Press.

Luborsky, L. (1976) Helping alliances in psychotherapy, in J.L. Cleghhorn (ed.) *Successful Psychotherapy*. New York: Brunner/Mazel.

Malan, D.H. (1979) *Individual Psychotherapy and the Science of Psychodynamics*. London: Butterworth Heinemann.

McGovern, J., Lindemann, M., Vergara, M., Murphy, S., Barker, L. and Warrenfeltz, R. (2001) Maximizing the impact of executive coaching: behavioural change, organizational outcomes, and return on investment, *The Manchester Review*, 6: 1–9.

Miller, A. (1979) *Das Drama des begabten Kindes und die Suche nach dem wahren Selbst*. Frankfurt am Main: Suhrkamp. Translated by Ruth Ward as *The Drama of the Gifted Child – The Search for the True Self*. New York: Basic Books.

Miller, S.D., Duncan, B.L., Brown, J., Sorrell, R. and Chalk, M.B. (2006) Using outcome to inform and improve treatment outcomes, *Journal of Brief Therapy*, 5: 5–22.

Mills, J. (2005) A critique of relational psychoanalysis, *Psychoanalytic Psychology*, 22(2): 155–88.

Mitchell, S.A. (1988) *Relational Concepts in Psychoanalysis: An Integration*. Cambridge, MA: Harvard University Press.

Mitchell, S.A. and Aron, L. (eds) (1999) *Relational Psychoanalysis – The Emergence of a Tradition*. Hillsdale, NJ: The Analytic Press.

Mor Barak, M.E.M., Travis, D.J., Pyun, H. and Xie, B. (2009) The impact of supervision on worker outcomes: a meta-analysis, *Social Service Review*, 83(1): 3–32.

Olivero, G., Bane, K.D. and Kopelman, R.E. (1997) Executive coaching as a transfer of training tool: effects on productivity in a public agency, *Public Personnel Management*, 26: 461–9.

Passmore, J. (ed.) (2011) *Supervision in Coaching*. London: Kogan Page.

Peterson, D.B. (1993) Measuring change: a psychometric approach to evaluating individual coaching outcomes. Paper presented at the annual conference of the Society for Industrial and Organizational Psychology, San Francisco.

Proctor, B. (1988) Supervision: a co-operative exercise in accountability, in: M. Marken and M. Payne (eds) *Enabling and Ensuring Supervision in Practice*. Leicester: Leicester National Youth Bureau and Council for Education and Training in Youth and Community Work.

Proctor, B. (2008) *Group Supervision*, 2nd edn. London: Sage.

Racker, H. (1968) *Transference and Countertransference*. New York: International Universities Press.

Ragins, B.R., Cotton, J.L. and Miller, J.S. (2000) Marginal mentoring: the effects of type of mentor, quality of relationship, and program design on work and career attitudes, *Academy of Management Journal*, 43: 1177–94.

Rapoport, L. (1954) The use of supervision as a tool in professional development, *British Journal of Psychiatric Social Work*, 2: 66–74.

Rogers, C.R. (1958) A process conception of psychotherapy, *American Psychologist*, 13: 142–9.

Rousseau, D.M. (1995) *Psychological Contracts in Organizations – Understanding Written and Unwritten Agreements*. Thousand Oaks, CA: Sage.

Sartre, J.P. (1957) *Existentialism and Human Emotions*. New York: Philosophical Library.

Schein, E. (1978) *Career Dynamics: Matching Individual and Organizational Needs*. Reading, MA: Addison-Wesley.

Schön, D. (1983) *The Reflective Practitione: How Professionals Think in Action*. New York: Basic Books.

Schroder, M. (1974) The shadow consultant, *The Journal of Applied Behavioral Science*, 10(4): 579–94.

Schwarzer, R., Mueller, J. and Greenglass, E. (1999) Assessment of perceived self-efficacy on the internet: data collection in cyberspace, *Anxiety, Stress and Coping*, 12: 145–61.

Scoular, A. and Linley, P.A. (2006) Coaching, goal-setting and personality type: what matters? *The Coaching Psychologist*, 2: 9–11.

Searles, H.F. (1955) The informational value of the supervisor's emotional experience, *Psychiatry*, 18: 135–46.

Sills, C. (2012) The coaching contract: a mutual commitment, in E. de Haan and C. Sills (eds) *Coaching Relationships*. Faringdon: Libri.

Simons, D.J. and Chabris, C.F. (1999) Gorillas in our midst: sustained inattentional blindness for dynamic events, *Perception*, 28: 1059–74.

Skinner, D. (2012) Outside forces in the coaching room: how to work with multiparty contracts, in E. de Haan and C. Sills (eds) *Coaching Relationships*. Faringdon: Libri.

Smither, J.W., London, M., Flautt, R., Vargas, Y. and Kucine, I. (2003) Can working with an executive coach improve multisource feedback ratings over time? A quasi-experimental field study, *Personnel Psychology*, 56: 23–44.

Stewart, L.J., Palmer, S., Wilkin, H. and Kerrin, M. (2008) The influence of character: does personality impact coaching success? *International Journal of Evidence-based Coaching and Mentoring*, 6(1): 32–42.

Stolorow, R.D. and Atwood, G.E. (1992) *Contexts of Being – The Intersubjective Foundations of Psychological Life*. Hillsdale, NJ: The Analytic Press.

Strachey, J. (1934) The nature of the therapeutic action of psychoanalysis, *International Journal of Psychoanalysis*, 15: 127–59.

Sumerel, M.B. (1994) Parallel process in supervision, *Eric Educational Reports*, April.

Tallman, K. and Bohart, A.C. (1999) The client as a common factor: clients as self-healers, in M.A. Hubble, B.L. Duncan and S.D. Miller (eds) *The Heart and Soul of Change: What Works in Therapy*. Washington, DC: APA Press.

Thach, E.C. (2002) The impact of executive coaching and 360° feedback on leadership effectiveness, *Leadership and Organization Development Journal*, 23: 205–14.

Torbert, B. (2004) *Action Inquiry*. San Francisco: Berrett-Koehler.

van Gorkum, F. (2007) *Dynamisch begeleiden in supervisie en coaching [Dynamic facilitation in supervision and coaching]*. Soest: Nelissen.

von Helmholtz, H. (1867) *Handbuch der physiologischen Optik [Handbook of physiological optics]*. Leipzig: Voss.

Wampold, B.E. (2001) *The Great Psychotherapy Debate: Models, Methods And Findings*. Mahwah, NJ: Lawrence Erlbaum.

Wilson, T. (2002) *Strangers to Ourselves: Discovering the Adaptive Unconscious*. Cambridge, MA: Belknap Press.

Index

Printed in Great Britain
by Amazon